Dear Else and Wayne,

Thank you
for being
who you are.
It has always
helped me.
　　Love,
　　　Aven

　　2010

Drawing A Life

A Manic Epic

By

Anca Dumitrescu

Drawing a Life - A Manic Epic

Anca Dumitrescu

Copyright 2010

All rights reserved. No part of this book
may be reproduced or transmitted
in any form or by any means, electronic
or mechanical, including photocopying,
recording, or by any information storage
or retrieval system, without permission
in writing from the publisher.

ISBN: 978-0-557-49531-3

To the sweet memory of what will be

1.

When my time at the Cooper Union was almost done I was becoming manic. My mother called me an ungrateful child because I would not return to her and to my father, and because I didn't feel right around them. I wanted to go to Europe for three weeks. My mother thought I was ungrateful and spoiled because she understood little of what I needed. She understands the solid reality she's used to; my own reality was too different. I was trying to prove to myself and to others that God is alive and that we're alive, through the use of art.

My sister said God is a dead concept. She spent time reading philosophy at school. To believe her or to believe what was said in Les Mots would have been for me to believe that there is no meaning and therefore no purpose to anyone, to painting or to any one painting whether it sold or not or charmed the critics or not. I had to know, before anything else would happen if the continuity I longed for was real. If not, there would be a little job for me somewhere, and I would take it. I had to know if a beautiful line stood for something somewhere.

I felt determination, which was more important than establishing safeguards or reassuring my parents that nothing was wrong when nothing was right. I had no time for these. I had only time to jump and hope in mid-jump that I'd land whole.

In the morning after I didn't take the plane to Frankfurt I was still there. Someone took me to her psychologist and I told her that all I wanted was a little rest. In the night, naked, I was praying for help, thinking God would appear as lover, out of the air. I felt benevolence all around me, not my mother's reality. I needed to give the way I knew how, through the body. I was desperate to allow God into that apartment. I hoped to be allowed to rest myself.

I told the psychologist all I wanted was some peace. I had too little to stand up to anyone with. But my father was driving in to take me back to New Jersey. I agreed because I wasn't ready to let go of my family and I wanted to be understood and loved. I thought I'd go back to Brooklyn after a few days.

My father came late and didn't see me. I was sitting on a step. My friend was already on her way to work. I sat reading the coffee cup that read It Is Our Pleasure To Serve You. Then I stuck my piece of green gum along the design and in that moment that action was a confirmation of trust. In that moment the word trust suggested itself and it was my confirmation of the existence of God.

After days of instability, for that moment, I felt well. That was unacceptable to psychiatrists later on. Psychiatrists are more rigorous than a thousand priests. When I looked up, my father was driving past me without seeing me. I stood up to meet him.

At Belleview, tied to a stretcher in the hallway, the young doctor pulled at my lids and said "How about a look at the real world now?" I had kicked my father, unwilling to leave with him from a lobby where he answered a call from his hospital. I wanted nothing to do with him when he pulled at me to go. I called him the Devil. The police came. I was handcuffed and brought to Belleview. I was given oxygen in the ambulance, tied to a stretcher and left temporarily in the hallway. While I lay in that hallway it was decided that I was a manic depressive.

With drugs, I became nothing. Everything started over. Later I read The Enormous Room and it made me think of this American sanity. When I woke up, there was somebody sitting at the door, waiting. The notes were going down on paper at regular intervals. Patient... I had time with my eyes closed to remember. I had time to know that I was not mad. After that I was alright. With a sadness that I was willing to show only to myself, it was alright to give signs of life.

Notes were taken. Showers were taken at six o'clock in the morning, little huts were built out of popsicle sticks. My homework was How I Will Change... There were ten more days for me on the ward while they adjusted lithium levels and sent me "home" in the care of my parents.

The old woman came from the doorway into the room. She asked me a question, and then another, while she wrote down what she saw. She told me to be a "good girl" so that peace would return to my parents. She went on to tell me about her family.

While my sister, my mother and my father sat in the room, I saw the line of insanity between us. The girl they knew was gone. I had come here into the hospital, and there was no returning. To them I was a wild animal and to me they were dead. Fear emanated from them. They didn't know what to say. I thought they should be looking at the sadness in my eyes, and seeing it. I felt that I might not be able to say anything to them ever again.

How could I claim madness or sanity? Only the line. For them this line didn't exist, because in psychiatric wards such reasoning is denial.

On the ward I kept my eyes open as logic came back to me as my ally. On a mental ward any action is incriminating. Logic returned so that I'd return to my life, outside. When I was manic, I knew so little as to say things out loud.

I had to start doing my assigned homework: How I'd Like to Be Different In The Future. My father pointed out that I had no friends, and when one came to the hospital to see me, he amended it to no friends but her.

I had enough life left in me that said No, I'm Not Dead, because being the cripple and settling in would have felt wrong. I had too many good little memories, like my fresh beautiful tomatoes in Paris after three weeks in Romania in 1988. That was returning to life too. There was the rain, and all the walking I'd done in the wet, welcoming streets. There were my little times of love, or love-like, nothing but this to help me along. I had my thoughts for friends.

I made collages out of ads in magazines. I did my homework of good intentions. I denied what I found out later might have a name: the astral plane. I was trained in logic from the beginning, and logic now said there was no explanation, that there wasn't even madness. But there was strong Evidence. The Western world as a whole said to me: Manic Depression, Chemical Imbalance; as if the two were one and the same. Period. Beginning and end. And who was I to argue? Acknowledge and succumb to your new self, said the entity of the doctor world, including my parents. But it was hard to think of lithium forever.

At school we either made or talked about art. Any of what we did could be art. We wrote poetry, took survey classes, and critiqued, during which time I became more and more serious with my own importance. I neglected money altogether, assuming that money, and the Way, would come, if I just kept on painting. Then I began to wonder if God exists. Then came the chemical imbalance. That changed my outlook towards money altogether: I tried to run from it.

With men, I've looked for a place to stop. I long for the bonding that would go to the core, if it could. That way I could lose myself. I could find a place to be, even if it's not my own. Why did it never occur to me then that there is a place of my own?

I've wanted to close my eyes and dig into an organic, deep corner of love, and be released. I haven't known how to stand still, but I do now. This is my life, this is how I am, and I can't be more until the next step. I'm finding more faith now and I'm grateful. Now I don't want to run. I'm tempted, a little, always. But the illusion of some other place doesn't make it past my first safeguard of reality.

When I took on manic depression, I took on the sense of failure, of not being enough. I lost the battle, my parents won. We'd fought over how I should live my life. I joined the struggle, trying to prove to them that I was making my own choices. They wanted me to be an artist, but when it came to how, I was supposed to be safe. In taking me "home" from the hospital in '89 they won.

My parents needed their daughter fixed, monitored and administered medication. They regained control, and used it. I was told, again and again, that there was something wrong with me, that my health was affected. I would have to modify my life into caution, and that what was wrong with me wasn't to be mentioned, especially the amoral sexuality. I refused my mother as a confidante, and she didn't like it.

I do believe, however, that it's possible for me to become crazy. Emotions, fear, and pain can cause chemical reactions. I say less these days. Words and thoughts pass through me and I let them go. They come so that I can let go of them. They may be spoken later, but not now.

I wonder if I will be what others think I'll be. This is a time with a lot to prove. But I need to be still, to allow words to pass through me. Words, thoughts, expectations, demands, fears - to see them and let them slip, as if the conversation were about somebody else. Or, when I am alone in the dark in bed to allow them time. Or in the field or the garden.

It's night, after some work in the yard. Everything melts into the bath. I've begun to forgive myself, to believe there's more. I want to live. I want to forget my arrogance. I want to be here where I am and be alive, to live out this little bit of peace inside me.

I was dreading the night alone because last night there was only the hole to sink into. But today I didn't fall into my gut, or my chest, or into pain. Tonight I didn't have to turn on every light. It's been a good day. For a couple of hours I managed to see nothing at all. I cut wood. I felt strong, and proud of my young body.

How do I find a mentor? I am still incomplete without one. I need guidance, a path to follow, a way to do what's required. My life is a mirage, other than the certainty of the physical, otherwise. Drugs don't manage to change the emptiness.

When the only thing available is a book, I start by staring at the page and saying to myself that it will take me somewhere for awhile. Then I fall into it. It's the same with movies, or a meal, or a walk.

I stand in this place I've retreated to and wish I'd stopped sooner and done less damage. I wish that I'd lived my life in the world, not on its edges. I've wanted to think I could destroy fear by identifying it; now I face it, but it's not going away.

I've wanted to run, and looked for a place to stop, in men. It's not the same with women, because it's understood that our bodies won't merge. But with men, I long for this bonding that would go to the core.

I need to begin to know for myself that it was alright to be so ill, and that I am healing. I need to start all over, and be kind and gentle to myself, not harsh and abrupt like I thought survivors and achievers ought to be. As to my loving intent, it got a bad reputation when it became all about sex. Then, it was important to please myself by pleasing others.

Love is no longer something that I think of as being found and held. Love is something as natural as our living bodies, a kind of breath of life. The urge is still there to lose myself in others, but that no longer means that I must deny myself, which it used to.

How do I describe my illness? Is it despair and joy all at once? I am frightened but I catch myself. I used to not catch myself, but fall deeper into pain, into hiding. I used to hide behind my smile.

When I fell apart, when I forgot to breathe deep, the hospital came rushing to meet me. It was always there, looming, threatening, proof of defeat. But my husband didn't disappear. He was and is still hurt, but he's here.

Is manic depression my death sentence, a cancer of the soul, or is it melancholy, elation beyond others' belief, through God's love? There's heresy in believing that one has been touched by God, and yet there it is. What is spiritual avowal is taken for spiritual arrogance.

Drugs bring balance. They bring the reassurance that is absent in my husband's eyes, because he is overwhelmed, unsure, unclear. I have released a creature of volatility, pain, and persistent optimism. Can it be as simple as living because every living cell tells me to live, not survive, or pretend, but live? Every moment, even in hesitation, has its time and purpose, and even more so now.

I left my husband, by bus, to go East again. He wasn't sure he could live with me this way, with my touch of God in every sentence. Now there's something more to calm the thoughts that ramble in my head. When I left, there hadn't been anything. In leaving, I avoided pain, sought comfort. It was more important to imagine I could leave than to allow for the pain.

I had New York in mind, Brooklyn, where I still had a friend who might put me up, and there were my parents to visit in New Jersey. I never made it. I cried on a sunny sidewalk in the middle of Winnipeg, in the middle of the afternoon, and that too was a step in my life, another mistake. Crying in public the way I did was a mistake. Well-meaning people took me to the police and the police took me to the psych ward. Well-meaning people everyone. But for a manic depressive there is just another notch, another hospitalisation, another episode.

Part of me would continue to cry because the recurrent factors continue to be drugs and hospitalisations. Those people who help you pass the time aren't allowed to touch you, or to be touched. It's not hospital policy. Errant sexual behaviour implies an errant person, a person who is wrong.

The rain is demolishing this house. It tries to demolish this house, to turn it over into grass, dandelions, ants and mosquitoes, back before the trailer, before we lived here. In the winter the snow on the roof pressed and squeezed it, making it leak in places into the relative warmth of the interior. I live in my mind, not in the grass like an insect.

The insects I see have definite jobs. I have another kind of definite awareness, one that slips into emotion, into confusion, one that to call it a definite thing would be stretching it a little. My jobs are jobs of my choice, given my skills and endurance, but my mind does more than weigh the task. It weighs, counts, listens, finds or does not find grace in the movement of the whole, and it weaves together stories, stories that explain, complicate or derail, set back on track; my mind is my own force of nature which demands to be tamed.

I walk around thinking about the things I no longer have and the people I no longer have. Despair allows for a way back. When I help the sage bush to be free of that part of it which is dead, it is also teaching me: it knows how to show me not to take too long, or to be too quick.

The dead bush no longer covers the center. I can stand in it like an oversized queen of sage bending in all directions to loosen what was old and dead away. My mind enters in correlation with the dead in my own heart, soul, mind. There, the connections remain traced beyond my control. The traces lead me back to the people I've known, even to imaginary ones, ones that I've only heard or read about. That's my reality.

I have the fear of not being, or not having enough to satisfy. This fear has sent me in and out of relationships; I want to give over my soul, to be spoken for, done, safe, told how to do it right. When it doesn't happen, I run back into being alone.

All around there's beautiful sunshine. The curtain turns the whole bedroom red. I am lying sick with the flu and trying to figure out how the extreme tiredness came about. How does the body feel sunk, and how does the mind lag? I move from here to there. Then I come to sit down at the table where I knew I'd find a pen. Here the sun makes it through the blind, onto my torso and head. In the old days I'd stay out of the sun because of lithium.

I go outside long enough to help my husband to hook up the bigger better power cable. I still wonder how it is with illness. My mind wavers and returns from a light nap. My body, as it breaks down, asks for patience. Now I can do what might have been impossible before: find patience. All the circuits and links are restored one by one. In one more day I'll be whole. One way or another I'll pass the bug and go on with my life. Nothing is lost. Time musing isn't lost. I am blessed. I'm loved, I'm alive.

I had a dream about my love sleeping with another woman and leaving me. I dreamt this in the middle of the night, and then again in the morning. Now when it's past noon I find strength to put aside my need for reassurance, for being told that I will not be left behind. This fear is like the air that fills the room, despite the sunshine and the snow outside.

I breathe, finding courage in powerlessness. I pray for love that isn't imposed on either side. It's the hardest thing I will have to do, to look through the nightmare and not believe that I'm something worthless, to be discarded. I have my own beauty which is worthwhile, one not based on fears of having to start out alone again.

I need to let my love grow, because I have work to do and love has everything to do with it. Pain and fear manifest in tears; I only have to know enough to go on. But I'm scared of the night. Not being a child makes that more serious.

What came was my own destruction. I tore down my life as I knew it: expanses of money, expanses of energy, of myself. Another manic state. Again, shedding of the old. What was most difficult for others to understand, for those not moving slowly enough to understand, was the natural sense of hesitation that entered my life then.

There was little left of the pain there used to be. Only regular pain, in my bones, and the pain of the separation and the coming back together again.

Pain is experiential. What I am granted for now, in the spring, is a fulfillment that comes with smell and sound. This fulfillment isn't mine, it belongs to my pores and marrow. It goes through. Not in, not out, but through. My life becomes a series of traces.

I came back from the hospital to a husband who doesn't yet understand the crazed beauty of my life, who can only imagine that there is always the chance that one day I'll be gone, but there is faith in both of us. Between God and insanity people will draw lines, if there's nothing to stop them. They often look for what's considered clean and no more. I stand firm.

I had the impulse again to run and fester. I was just out of the hospital, with a fear as palpable in my stomach as the flu. I'd been powerless to stand and scream out my collective demons. But with a home to come back to it was different - a man of my own, who'd worried, and the home itself. Something in me wanted me to run, with the old impulse of pulling a geographic.

It started with a seminar on spiritual growth. My husband went in January and I went in February. I wasn't supposed to at all, but when my husband got back he insisted on my going. While at this seminar, I became manic and had sex with two of the men in my group. It was part of my plan of saving the world. What I did instead was wreck what there was of my new life, which ultimately meant that I had to start over. Destruction became part of regeneration.

In the hospital, there were particulars: Anca Dumitrescu. Edmonton area, born January 29, 1967, in Constanta. Romania, immigrated to the United States on December 29th. 1979. Education - Cooper Union School of Art, New York... Languages - French, Romanian. Italian... Work - mailroom clerk, telephone operator, girls' camp in the mountains, life drawing model. My fortune cookie read *Relaxation Is Deserved*.

2.

In the warmth of the waiting room all is forgotten. The run from the car, inside, slides into the recent past and the background. The woman switches from arthritis to crossed legs to sugar, with the man across the small room.

Last night I didn't go. Luckily I didn't have to.

Now it's salt.

It's good to be out of my own mind.

The guy at the convenience store offered to clean my parents' house for me. I told him it's already clean except for Rosie's peeing and dumping everywhere. I will see the endocrinologist soon. They called the woman with the hopeful tone, like one who believes. In what?

Do I really need more money to be free? Yes, but it's one of those chicken and egg things. I need not to worry about how much this pad costs, or about how I will get through the month on forty dollars. It'll happen.

Everybody here has debt, low income or not. But the doctors here in this lousy office with a two-hour waiting time are good. I will no longer believe my mother when it comes to health. I got too sick this last time, and a year and a half ago. With the new psychiatric medication I will come down a notch.

The fluorescent light overhead has the disturbing buzz everyone is used to. Light comes through the window, the screen across from me advertises medication and two people are standing, drug company representatives. They will get in soon enough. There is the give and take. There is someone back there now. Hermann is somewhere in the back of my mind, reminding me that there is something normal about me, that I am not a plaything.

I will write what I like about myself. It is harmless enough. When the time comes I may become diplomatic, though in this respect it is not in my nature to do so. The important thing is to make the break with my parents, which Hermann agrees with. I don't remember, he might not have said that exactly, but only that my parents would like to know that I will be alright in New York, so that I need to use one of my talents if not all, to speak with actions. With help, more will happen.

The fear of not being enough or being able to rise beyond what I feel stays, sometimes, though I no longer feel beaten. I have been the sick one, pitied and coddled. The current sense of superficiality will pass, but I don't want it to pass into mania. I fear not being able to be anything but manic or depressed. That makes me feel useless in a way I can't bear. I've wanted to please, to be useful.

John put his arms around me, leaned his head heavily on my shoulder and swayed. How come you have such a thin back, he said. I remember that. His wrists were raw, across not up. He made me a belt in the arts and crafts class.

I was angry with him because I didn't understand. He has a twenty-year-old son now, the reason he went back to Montana and married and settled in.

I don't know, last I heard he was playing in a band, maybe with his wife. Maybe we ate ice cream out of a gallon container, with our fingers, with each other's fingers. Maybe we took a walk for a long time in the middle of the night, north of Columbia, to find a store open that sold condoms, since neither of us had assumed. Maybe we kissed on film.

We kissed when he came back, loaded with lithium, finishing the semester. We kissed in a side office of one he was working in. He said I was an angel, that he would find his way into my bed in Paris. I was getting ready to go there on exchange. He was dreamy, he was hanging on for that last kiss. I wasn't listening. I didn't listen, for so long. I was already getting high on concepts and varnish. I was no more than taking in information, nothing more than taking notes to fit into the work.

I am faced with crazy-making behaviour just walking in the door. Sit down, and again, and again. The tension attached to domination reeks in the room, and the house. Confrontation is looming as soon as I am there. Everything deadens until I turn on the radio, feed the cats, move about the space. My father sits like a man condemned, which he is, grasping at me. He wants my details. He has always wanted them and now, when he is no longer able to be truly bullish about it I no longer give them to him. Or maybe it isn't being bullish, just that I have learned to let him slide off me.

My father is obsessed with my sitting down in a chair. He's not getting anything out of me standing, maybe if he can get me to sit he can extract a fact out of me. Good luck. I ask how he is, he returns to his mission. I seek the comfort of the glass of Pepsi. Or the half-full, the third even. It's my gin. I hear a little something I want to get down.

My father isn't a warlock any more than my mother is a witch, but he does come up for air at times in his sea of dementia, if that's what it is, with details about my recent stay away. Now he wants to know if I'd like to live in Switzerland, and I refuse to answer, without a word.

It hasn't been too long since I've acquired this tool of not answering without actually being rude. It seemed rude when my sister did this with her nanny over a question about her daughter, but now I have this tool too, thanks to her. I don't have to answer, and I don't have to volunteer. This is priceless reckoning, and we must all come to it in our own good time.

Fear stands with me tonight. I am in my safe hole. I have come in from the cold, I may make no more mad gestures, and grow my hair. I am apologizing, however. In a transition it is alright to apologize only a little, and keep going.

I may not always be in this state of aloneness. It is good to reconsider my options, some of which I never dreamed I had. The pattern has shifted; writing is what makes me well now, not just the others. I have the tools, and I know the murky waters. They're mine, after all. All the textures and smells and appeals are mine, and things change. I take what I have learned and walk away.

Hermann is the first man who has made it into the den. I didn't even realize it. He came to run the marathon and broke the spell. Until then, I had been so ashamed of my parents that I would not allow anyone I wanted in my life romantically, to meet them. Tom, my boyfriend in high school, was right, they were too much to deal with.

One night my mother sat him down interrogation-style and drove him away from me with questions like, So, are you thinking about marrying her or what? When I got home that night, when I heard my mother in her own voice say that if he wasn't able to take that much he was no good for me, I shut down, and have been that way since. Hermann changed that, unwittingly or on purpose. At this point it doesn't matter.

       The pattern continued until last night, when I hit a painful block over it. It hadn't registered how painful it really was. This morning Tony helped me realize that it was Hermann who broke the spell. He gets all the credit, by sneaking in the back door and freeing me. Now I will do whatever he asks me. I am writing, I am eating more, I am daring to exist.

       When we wandered down the hill, taking black and white pictures with the camera he chose for me, he watched and kept his distance. I didn't know what to make of it, and as in New York I kept going with faith in civility, so grateful for the opportunity to act like a regular human being. At dinner, I felt taken into a world that might just be wonderful.

       But at coffee, in the hotel lobby with high ceilings, on the couch for the better part of an hour, my heart was breaking at having to leave this man the next morning, this man who was entirely proper, as he should have, under the circumstances. Then I slept on his bed, like a baby, in my loose pyjamas, while he slept on the couch, and I woke up surrounded by buildings as comfortable with each other as they had to be, given the city setting, in the morning light; we had breakfast like new old friends. So yes, I would do anything for this man.

My mother and I are experiencing what in Recovery would be called a temperamental deadlock. I have debased myself over the years so frequently to try to win, to win her over, to prove her wrong, to take away the sceptre she clings to. But that is all imagination, a prolonged imagination on fire, as they would say again in Recovery.

My mother is a woman, not a witch, as I have thought of her in my psychotic times. Yes, there have been those times, I admit to it. I have left the rational at times and lived the stuff films are made of, crossing America, crossing Canada, trying to hitchhike to Canada again before it occurred to me that I might as well stand it for one day and use my plane ticket.

After so many years, my mother and I are still going through the same thing. Paper money is just more important, and so be it. Now, my challenge is to find self-worth. I know very well that I can't engage in any more struggles, and that I must disentangle manic depression, with its neurological, physical, and emotional aspects, from guilt, shame, and the sense of loss.

It was the fall of '99, while I was working in New York guiding as small group of printers in an good black and white lab which has since gone digital. Dan had helped me find someone to help me cope with my intense depression. I had painted my small apartment in Brooklyn a light wine colour and had run out of things to do. I had long gotten rid of the bulk of the art work I had brought with me from Canada and from New Jersey. There was nothing to distract me, and no money. Again, that. I was in love with Dan, but we kept our distance.

I asked my mother for the money for the therapy, she agreed, and it was worth it, but early in November she pulled the plug. She said he had over-charged her on one bill. That later turned out to be incorrect. The cut-off made the depression so intense that I shifted directly into mania. That is how it works, in my case. There is mounting depression, a willingness to die without the intent to do it, and the shift into the power of anger and daring I would never have normally.

I got on a train to California. I wanted to meet Robert Redford, and possibly Brad Pitt. Those two are still connected in my mind somehow. Meeting Robert Redford has been a theme in my manic times, a pleasant and harmless one I think. Once I made it to Santa Monica.

I got on the train and by the time I reached Chicago in the morning I had thrown away all my ID. And I had been with a porter all night, someone who seemed to me a prince right out of the Arabian Nights, so smooth and agile and more. That was the end of the ride and the beginning of another hospitalisation, when I turned myself in to the police.

The hospital was somewhere outside of Chicago. There I dared kiss a fellow inmate on the lips and was put in restraints for it for some time. My mother came to get me. We had to take the train back because I couldn't fly without ID and I got to see the porter again, who was embarrassed but glad to see I was alive and in my right mind again. We kept the night between us.

All this time, years, inertia rules my life. I must keep my word to myself now. People care, and I am forced to care, because of the shock of the physical proximity. Words spoken, streets and cobblestones and museums walked across together so that the time would come for me to wake up to my own lacking. Not meanly, but decidedly. When I look at my niece and would tell her things, would lift her up, I forget, if it occurred to me at all, that there are others who would lift me up, who would teach me and show me compassion, to start with. I too look from face to face for the immediate, since it is still the quickest way. But the face may be tired, or guided by restraint, so that messages become mixed despite all good will.

What interests me most is communication. I will stay with that. I did assume in the past that I know someone from his speech, his countenance, his deeds that I know of and accomplishments. But I know more, now. There is no knowing a person until the physical entering of someone's space. Things get glossed over much of the time.

Why was there a sheet with a hole in it on the guest bed? Why was there an insistence on food, throughout this last visit in Europe. I have been so alone in my life that I am put off by next to nothing.

My dark windows make me think now of Hermann with the light of day shining in. I have been much the opposite. Can the darkness in my home literally have to do with my dark state? Maybe. That means that I have to change this too. Is that right? I haven't replaced the blinds that won't roll up, after more than a year, with the reasoning that I can't afford it. That comes up again, scrimping again.

I always did creep into the shadows of the darkroom as if it were home. Why? I was so much in the sun, so many years ago. There are answers here that I am blind to for lack of use or exposure. In a reverie I would say that everyone knows the outcome but me. Or, that I am pushing my way through life, and will be doing more so. Things are in flux, so that the outcome changes with each move I make.

For now the one thing to focus on is staying with the resolve to change, with the idea, if nothing more, that things can change in my life. I am the big car who thinks I'm a little car, as Hermann put it, and the transition is difficult. However, the thought is planted in my head and I must prepare for it as if for a race, and then run it. It will come through the writing. This is my weapon, which I have been so afraid to use because of repercussions. My curtains are thick as drapes. I don't want "them" looking in, but it's time to shed.

        I've learned so much here in the dark, I've made friends, things mean something so that any foray into the light is fruitful, I long to stay, but Hermann won't let me. He wants me out, doing something, eating, God knows what else. It is painful to be cared for in this way.

        Demetri was one of the ones I wouldn't bring home. He made fun of me, of my soft drinks. No one had taken photographs of him in a long time until he let me, before my long trip east with the trailer full of framed photographs for the show, and the ice storm. Blue was half grown by then and running around without a collar in Seba Beach, where I lived in Canada, where I had my studio. He would try to hump me sometimes at night and I kept telling him he was just a dog, which made him grunt and go away.

        In January I threw my own birthday party and Demetri came, in his old car. He was studying to be an engineer, a few years younger, and unattainable. He had a girlfriend in Europe. That made him safe. I've never been with anyone taken. But he came, and although his parents owned a restaurant, he liked my soup.

The illusion of safety lies thin over my mother, but it is enough for her. She thinks I write when I'm on the edge, ready to dive, ready to lose it, as opposed to when I begin again to straighten out lazy thoughts and nerve endings. She is part of the illusion of men and women, the illusion of safety in numbers, in the heated apartment and the paid rent. The fear of expression that cannot be dominated by her, frightens her. She will not allow for it, but here I am, telling her I'm alright.

Suffering is the key to understanding, but in the meantime there has to be something that might bring salvation, if there are to be more than a waste of life or radiant sparks, which can destroy the source and often lose their effect. There has to be something to let me climb back out of the hole, if only to be able to tell about it. This is what it's come to, for me, the telling of it, the climb out of the hole, laying aside the penetrating incapacity to show one's beauty, or by any other name.

Having fallen over the edge many times, I know that safety is an illusion, but I can work in the warmth of the apartment now, have my needs met, without falling into mud. The heaviness is overwhelming but it's not impossible to overcome. Let it be mud, then. Inertia works both ways. An expert at falling off can go a long way.

All the things that have come together in my home, in my apartment, have come together for a reason. A scroll, a hat rack, books, a pretend old bed, newspapers, more books, dishes without food in them, in the kitchen. I have new neighbours, all the bills are paid on time, and there is the smell of tea in the cup on the floor. All these things have come together for a reason. They need to ground me, and they do.

I am unaccustomed to love, though it may come again. But grounding is reality, as much as anything is. I can't do without it. Joe's shop burned down but his things are with me, the quilt, the spoon rest, my Bars of Ireland T-shirt.

My books I mostly look at, for fear of flooding my mind with vivid images which I will not be able to erase. Books may as well be movies for me. But it is comforting to know that these worlds are there around me in the room. Sometimes I reread the ones I already read, like I see movies I've already seen. There's a world around me and there is a lot of darkness and emptiness in it. I need focus for other things, like this writing now.

It is these things, in the daylight hours, that make it work. The fury of working at night hasn't started yet. This is the preparation. Again, the grounding. My things may not cost much, and they are not alive like Josie is alive, made of fur and belly and powerful muscles, but I can't wait to see them nonetheless.

There was a garden every morning when I woke up, from when I was about eight till twelve. There were men in it, boys really, who loved me, who were teaching me the art, deep in the grass. I would go, climb the wall of the real, find myself there, not wanting to go back to the world of the everyday.

They were preparing me for the end of the path in the garden, where their most trusted of all lay still, nearly dead. They let me know that it was up to me to go to him, to wake him. The morning I did, it was all over, the wall disappeared, the garden, the rest. I didn't know what to do. I had no choice but to let go.

Four years ago the question that used to come to mind was why I get so shy with men I fall in love with that I go find the first man available to chew up and discard, physically, instead of making an attempt of any kind to make myself and my feelings known. That was then. I have let go of that debate within myself since. It isn't just manic behaviour. I've always done it. My self-esteem was lacking.

I dove to a lower level time and again, where I would have almost certain success and no emotional involvement initially; it was perfect, in a self-destructive sort of way. It had to do with shame of my family, embarrassment to such a degree. In time I will unlearn it, now that it no longer matters.

It was three weeks into the pregnancy when I had the abortion. It was supposed to be safe, at the very end of the cycle, and it was very hard for me to get pregnant because my womb is split in two. But it happened. Jared was very much in love. He didn't know or understand my pattern of letting go of love. We had gone to beginners' acting class, in the fall of '90. I'd run away from a relationship in Europe. I'd had a show that went nowhere and cost my parents money.

The aborting took me into a deep depression. I'd had a little job making sandwiches which I quit, and moved back to my parents' from Brooklyn, which made me more depressed. They had said I could have the baby but I'd have to stay with them for the next fifteen years. The thought of that destroyed me.

That April I swung the other way after helping out with a student film production and ended up meeting my hero of the acting world, the author of The Empty Space, in Romania of all places. I wanted to buy a house with a garden on the outskirts of Bucharest for five thousand dollars and stay there, but my mother came to get me and there was another hospitalisation.

Being with my parents, I feel empty and disconnected. I've felt this way for twenty years and tried to understand, to make it better, or to make it worse so the bubble would burst. I tried to attach myself to others and their relationships so that my life would seem or be filled with their lives. It doesn't matter how or when in the end - I'm one of the lonely people.

The one person I felt connected to was my grandmother. She knew me since I was a little girl, and nurtured me. She was the mother my mother didn't have time to be because she was working too hard. Nonna took me on trains, to the milk and bread lines, took me to her card parties, took me to church and asked me to always to light a candle for her when I went in one after she was dead. I still do that. It's important to have that dollar.

That's mostly what I knew of religion, because we weren't allowed to speak about it in Communist Romania. Nonna knew what to do, even when my parents left and never came back. She had her doubts, it turned out, but she didn't tell me or my sister. And she came to the States, leaving my uncle Kiki behind, a little while later.

When I was a teen, just being younger was bad enough. My sister was the beautiful one, I wasn't. But over the years, both my mother and my sister have gained weight, which to them is very important. My mother now goes on and on about how old and fat she is. Yet she compares herself to me still, every day, in the way she dresses, in the way she looks. My father, who is a lecherous bastard to the end, says he looked my chest up and down because he likes the way I look. Others, those I look forward to, tell me I look young, sometimes beautiful, and often glowing.

I look into my life and each part of it comes to meet me. I flow with it, it flows with me. In this black and white world, stories continue. The green keys are my continuation, as if I'm pushing nature itself into words. Nature lives, the transition is complete. As far as photography goes, that was my point - that essence does, and does not, live in the camera. If there's no touch to guide it, the essence sleeps. It remains. What is of the essence waits, in the camera, as it does in the body.

When I dig into myself I find the source, the place where faith is abundant. I go there purposefully. First I had to go everywhere else, to be always on the outside, until I realized there were always more places to run to and away from. That has ended.

It's a Sunday of contentment. I have tried so hard, I have put up with enough, now I will not be pushed around, and this I will do gently, ever so gently, letting things slide off. What better way. The wave came, I rose with it, I learned what some people were capable of and some weren't, and I learned how much love I am capable of myself. Then the wave came down again, and I am grateful for the connection with the real.

My favourite story from creative writing class at Cooper was the tree and the fly story. There was a tree, far off in the distance from anything, anybody and any other tree. But there was a fly living in it, whom the tree treated the best it could because it was the only living thing there.

One day, dissatisfied, the fly told the tree that it would go off to the city because it was bored. The fly had a cousin there who lived on a wall and had a very interesting time of it.

No matter how the tree pleaded, the fly had made up its mind. But as it opened its mouth to say good-bye birds of all kinds started to fly out of it, to the amazement of both the fly and the tree. As they kept coming, the tree said to the fly, Now you have to go to the city and be a fly on the wall! The fly shut its mouth and flew away.

I don't know what to do with power, other than not take it, or not use it if I don't know the rules. When I used to feel powerless there was the other extreme: knowing that the struggle could only bury me deeper, that the only thing to do is to slow it down so that it's less painful, waiting for the release which always comes.

Having power means using it well. It is not an option. I can't forget to do the job well "just this once." The attempt, at least, has to be constant - continuous improvisation and openness. Life is the ultimate game. But with the thought once formed there is no more loafing. When the power comes to me now I pass it on, then there's more power, and more love.

They call it obsessive compulsion. I call it being prepared when there is no choice but to be, when there are no extra sips of one's pleasure. It was past one o'clock in the morning. I was lucky that I was driving the standard, not the truck. It was snowing heavily and there was a big dip over a hill, with tracks enough for one, and two cars were stopped together at the bottom, arguing over a small accident, maybe. I shifted down all the way and stayed on the road. It would have been easy enough for them to move when I honked the horn, in the stillness, but they didn't.

I wasn't afraid. In those days I wasn't afraid, and I knew how to drive those roads. David, my husband, had gone home in the truck hours earlier. Now it was dark. I had been in a scene in a show that got cancelled. For an extra, they went to great trouble to put me in a gorgeous outfit for the night of the dance. It fit. More than that.

We waited for hours, as extras do. The main scene was shot early. There was a man there, the best dancer of all, who needed a partner for one of those step dances people learn early, up there, and they picked me, who had no idea. I kept up in a way of my own, staying with the gaze of this man and my back straight. My feet found their way. It was all wrong, but it worked. David said it was all wrong. He played the drummer in the band. I pulled back on the road.

I could have taken the main road and the highway, I don't know why I took the back way. After I passed through the strait of the two cars, I did get on the highway, and just at the left turn, across the highway from where we lived just off the road, the car stalled, with its nose in the opposing fast lane. A tractor trailer was coming some distance away.

There I was, so I did what a confident or a very foolish person would do, knowing the truck couldn't stop that short. I got out, held the door open and pushed, in my workman's boots you're supposed to wear up there in a snow storm, and the car made it, and so did I, and so did the truck. Now, fear lives with assurance by its side. They do not quarrel over me. They stand watching, merely. They know that I will choose one or the other at any given moment and stand at attention.

I turn another year older and more aware of both fear, in its familiarity, and acceptance, in its quiet wrenching affirmation. I have come to a time in which I know I have choices to make and that I have to make them. I have come to know what withdrawal is like.

Most people don't generally have their needs satisfied, which makes me ask, why should I? Is it possible for me to just get through the day, drive somewhere, be there awhile, share slivers of communication while I'm there, drive back, go shopping, come home, watch TV, eat, do the same thing the following day?

Recognition within the humdrum universe makes things worse if its only result is to promote the status quo. Maybe it's a contradiction, to think of awareness as holding on to the past or a limited present. Recognition is awareness, but in glimpses, which is very frustrating. There is no helping it though, a person has to go through the process, with a lot of faith in the unexplained.

When we moved to my husband's land one thing that made me happy more than all else was Wes' road. Wes was the neighbour up the hill. He's moved now, and I don't know what happened to his road. But I do know what I felt then. In the winter it was the flat stretch I welcomed cross country, because I didn't ski very well. In the summer it was the place to walk down slowly, down to Art's place, with the horses that loved rose hips in the fall. But in the summer, in the early summer especially, it was that road, only without the boys, without the wall, without the man. There were cows up the hill to the right and woods and thickets farther on. It was the road, in daylight.

I used to need men as shelter from loneliness. Sex was easy because I came on to them and generally they didn't turn me away. My driving hunger for both mental stimulation and intimacy is something that stays. I dismiss men, I dismiss myself. It takes forever and it is excruciatingly painful to trust anyone, to become friends, which is the only way with me, if there's a chance it will last.

Rape sums it up, but it must be explained. It was my first hospitalisation, at UMDNJ in Newark. I had been transferred from Belleview in New York. UMDNJ was 'my father's' hospital. He worked there as a surgeon. While under observation in the first few days there, in May of 1989, a fellow patient, a man, took me by the hand and into a bathroom and raped me.

I was high, on a natural manic high, I was stunned and did not scream. Moments later, I was told, staff came in and pulled the man off me. I had been frozen, I had not screamed. That was later used as 'evidence' that the act was consensual. I was taken into a room where it was discovered that I had been menstruating and therefore lesions were impossible to determine. I was given an AIDS test, although I knew the HIV takes six months to manifest. Then I was cuffed.

The man on the other hand was free to walk the corridor and look in on me through the open door. They waited with the Haldol until the next morning when my father came in. He was furious. He said that if I wasn't willing to sue the hospital it meant that it hadn't been rape after all. Two days later I woke up from the daze and the man was walking the hallway, looking in. I simply couldn't face a trial.

Then a campaign started on behalf of the staff, as to the guy being deranged and not being able to stand trial, but more importantly, my not telling my boyfriend because he wouldn't want me anymore, because I would lose him. That worked. I never did tell him and lived with the shame.

When it comes to the medications I'm taking, I'm understanding that I'm the only one who really knows what's going on. I have to let the doctors know, and I do, but I'm the one who has to know what's too much, when, and why. It's a funny position to be in to know oneself so well. I'm used to knowing myself well, but not in that sense. Or maybe I have always known myself in that sense too but I haven't thought of it as a job before. It is my job to pay attention to what happens to me. It's something so basic, but it's taken me all this time and this period of clarity, to get this far.

The body being gradual, it returns to the self gradually. Pimpled, scarred, grown, trim, it returns. The troops fall in. I tell myself that I am alive, and live, I hear the rhythms in the cars' passing on the highway. These are moments of change, moments, weeks, sacred blocks of time. There's continuity to be preserved through focus, living with continually less distraction of purpose, being in plain sight without the distraction that used to happen.

Waves of insecurity come and go as I think of all my manic purges. There's something right about not getting attached so much to things, just experiencing the essential, and carrying that inside me, as if the presence of a new life. I have only myself in a sense, in this doubting mood. It passes, then it comes back. How perfect do I have to be, and for whom? It's as if there will be a line I will have to cross to be finally "okay." There's the strong sense that I'm not there yet. I'm at the beginning of this trip.

What appears to be an outer danger is an inner threat. Again from Recovery. It fits here, the threat of not being enough. Always someone else to please. This is the line to cross, and it may come into reach yet, with a little luck and a lot of work, breaking the cycle, reaching the point, finally, at which it's alright to be who I am. What is dawning on me is that no matter what I do accomplish, my illness is still there and there's no point getting angry about it. Recovery in general is the most I can have on my agenda right now.

My mother asked me about calendars. I don't know how long it's been since I've had one. The last one I remember was of wolves, some beautiful black and white photographs of wolves. Even then, maybe because the prints were so beautiful, it seemed to me that no one should photograph wolves ever again, that they should be left alone. I am a mother wolf myself, waiting to be left alone.

Robert, the one I had the manic night with five years ago, had that drawn look, sunken cheeks of a runner and survivor. He'd had three heart transplants already. I still don't remember anything about that night. I took off all my clothes, and I asked him to lead me by the hand into the bedroom. That was it, and waking in the morning.

Nicole, my nearly three-year-old niece, is in danger of ending up on a calendar for being so beautiful. How I wish I could keep her from that, but it may be impossible because she lives not only in a different country but in a labyrinth of an emotional sort, finding her way through the expressions on the faces that surround her.

She doesn't always make it, indeed there are often barriers and blocks. But she has the strength of ten men when it comes to recognizing what is wrong with her world, which makes her seem spoiled. But she is guarding her kingdom, that fierce little soul deep inside her. I love her, I long to guide her through some of it, but I have to let go, as with everything else, and hope that she hangs in there like I did until I thank God my eyes were crossed all of a sudden at the age of four and from then on I spent all my spare time with my grandmother, going to the clinic. I hope to be that person for her.

How do I stay on a path when everywhere there are distractions? To be aware of having a path at all involves some responsibility. Awareness is both inborn and developed. It can be dormant or frustrated for what seems like ages, but given the slightest forward jolt it will begin to take part in one's life. It comes from somewhere, awareness, this thing that is so closely tied to intuition. I am aware so much of the time, of my own life, of others' and find myself hitting walls of frustration, sometimes at disconcertingly short intervals. But sometimes, when I'm alone, a wave of warmth washes over my neck and into my chest, and is gone.

3.

I ask myself again - where to begin. The past few days remind me of back in July of '94 when, after having been manic and in and out of the hospital since March, I finally accepted that my husband and I would split up. That, although my parents didn't want me back. I was going back to them. I ended up staying, but the acceptance came when I was finally helpless and released at the same time. Like I'd sunk low enough for it not to matter anymore, but in a good way.

Now I've sunk again, maybe to the same depth, maybe lower. Another good two years and then this. A home, school, work, a car which meant and means independence, but which is having trouble again, and is parked for now until I can spend money on it. Which means that I drive the car my mother bought for me to drive and swallow my pride. Most of all the trouble now is duality, now that I know what duality is, about how much I should allow myself to be emotionally dependent right now, on anyone. Duality in general.

My parents, my mother especially, thinks that my behaviour can and should be curbed, or that it should have been curbed by now. I appreciate the help they offer and say no more. This saying no more is a problem in itself, though. I'm so used to it. Not only do I say little but sometimes it takes all the energy I've got not to leave the room or the building. I have been leaving a lot. Not that I have something better to do but I just want to get away, to find a corner to crawl into, which isn't easy either.
I may never own a home, have children of my own, or be fully responsible for myself financially. I have to live with that possibility. My longings as far as that goes may never be fulfilled and as of now I may be in debt for a very long time. But I have to turn at least that last bit around, thinking positively about my ability to work.

In the past few days my mother has stepped in to help again, but at a cost. Domination in the guise of service reigns. My huge phone bill is an example. She will help me with that too, but with her approval only. I no longer have long distance at all and no calling card, and my collect calls are blocked because I accepted several from a homeless man I met in New York the last time I was there. Once again I am fenced in, as it is clear that I need to be. But feeling fenced in is exactly the reason this last prolonged episode started in the first place.

That is what I have to change - this outlook of being fenced in. Somehow back in Alberta I was able to do that, at least for awhile. I was there on the land with no transportation, just the garden and the field and Wes, our neighbour, and I was able to accept that everything was gone, with maybe not a little hope in the future.

This isn't the field, and things are more complicated because of the debt. But I have to hope that that ease that I long for will come in its own time, even if it means severe limitations, self-imposed or otherwise, and a lack of independence. In Recovery terms I'd say I have temper at the illness, instead of seeing that it's fate-appointed, not self appointed.

Sometimes I just don't know what to do. I no longer feel like I can ask for help from my parents, financial or otherwise, because they both, my mother especially, tend to dominate me as best as they can. This I understand, because the more she gets a sense that there is something wrong with me, the more she feels she is in the right to lead her life in her own irresponsible way. I do what I can to abstain from my epic outbursts, but I am beginning to see that at best I can tone them down, and that without close monitoring such as in that of a spouse, for example, or even then, would they be able to held down to a minimum.

What I return to though, is this neediness and loneliness. Even as I'm able to express it, I wonder if I'll ever be able to do more than that. I generally shy away from interaction, with potential friends and lovers. Partly I'm afraid of disturbing their lives with my highs and lows and partly I'm afraid of the pain of rejection, of abandonment. I could think about how this all started till my dying day and it might not help, or at least not heal the pain that comes persistently in wave after wave. I wish and I pray that one day I will be able to stop beating myself up, like my therapist says, and move on.

Meanwhile I still feel like I'm hanging on by a thread, beyond the everyday act of showing up. I seek companionship in the radio and TV and movies, and bury myself altogether in what might be. At least for now. I have withdrawn, at least for now. It's no good and I know it.

Sometimes it still seems to me that I can't truly function and accept my mental illness at the same time, because the stigma is that great. As much as I'm working on acceptance, the waves still come. I see my illness itself as an insurmountable handicap when I feel like this, instead of as a limitation. I seek acceptance outside of myself, still. Why is it that in my mind there's still so much to prove?

But that's it. I need to please. I need to be accepted. That's what achievement has always been about. Now I'm standing still so I can stop this, finally, and I'm anything but comfortable. I'm afraid.

Insecurities creep right back in. I don't know how long it will take for this to dissipate once and for all. How many friends should have to tell me that they're standing by me. Obviously this has to come from the inside.

Despite everything, I still would run to my parents for approval. But I know better now, since it's become very clear that our interactions are attempts at satisfying needs, not at interaction in the true sense. It is expected that I will call, that I will make the first move, and that I am the needy one. They need so much themselves but they don't ask. If they take anything, they take it for granted. And here I am still tormenting myself with how to make it right. After all this time, pain, fury, etc. And I don't want any more of it. I want to be excused from this charade. It all hurts too much.

I know there's a reason for this. I just don't know what it is. I have to trust that this is more of the process I have to go through. I have to know that it's not massage work or any other work in its financial respect that's going to make me accept myself.

Maybe I'm close to acceptance, and that's why I feel so confused, about self-expression most of all. That sort of makes sense to me. It's as if I'm giving up another layer of my ego, however that sounds. Maybe the feeling of acceptance that does come frequently enough is and will continue to be part of my duality. I am torn so much of the time about just about everything anyway. And I always feel like it's up to me to "fix it." No wonder my manic highs included the need or the urge to save the world in one respect or another. I always thought it was my responsibility.

I'll have to insist on telling myself that it's not up to me to save the world, to remind myself that I have an excessive sense of duty and responsibility. To stop trying to be so pleasant when I feel anything but, to walk away sometimes and know that it won't mean that I'll be suspected and put away for being less than congenial. I think, after all, that I'm still afraid of my parents, of what they could do to me, of what they have done. They still have that hold over me, that I have to be good and prove myself. To them. I don't know what to think about that. I'm too tired to go at it for another round. I won't. I'll just let it go. But it will take time, so I have to give it all the time it takes.

At home, I do my meditation. I do laundry and iron. I cook the most basic of meals when I'm not eating sandwiches. I listen to music. I just spent the last week writing because I needed to, not with intention of publishing yet. I now watch great movies on cable, mostly on the Sundance channel, and, this week I've started swimming again, which feels great, at twenty laps a session, at a slow, even pace.

I keep in touch with my women friends to some extent, though I wait until the urge builds. This I do over the phone, very little in person, and through e-mail. This little stretch is one of prolonged hesitation. I have the impulse, which is old and familiar, to prove something again, by way of getting "a real job," for example, whatever that may mean. But I have more sense than to try, because during the few days in which I was busy these past months I got tired, worn out and stressed out much more easily than ever before. I work best, now, in small concerted efforts, not in long or otherwise draining hours. So I do have, to some extent, a handicap. It can't be helped, and I'm beginning to accept that.

When I see myself rested, well, and willing, as I am this morning, I get the pressing feeling that I could be useful somewhere somehow. I get the feeling that I'm not doing enough, that I should be making efforts, outside friendships, at furthering my social life. And yet I know, decidedly, that this is a period of transition, once again, and that I must be patient. I've done my writing, I've done my schooling, I am working, a little, and it's okay.

But this helplessness lingers. This may be a new threshold, one that is at the tip of my tongue, in a sense, but I can't get it out yet. So, patience, I have to leave it there. Does it make any sense? When I am outside of my little world I am more busy noticing people's behaviour than ever, even my own. Women's casual conversations in the locker room at the pool or at the nail salon seem blatantly explicit to me. I don't know if I'm just old-fashioned beyond belief or if I just never learned to relax and think in terms of casual conversation. Though I do that, with my friends. I don't know. I do my best when someone includes me, and let it go at that. It would be safe to say I'm a private person. That can't be the worst thing to be.

Last night talking to my therapist, something was confirmed which I'd been thinking about. Two things, actually. One, that I go manic partly to become dependent and get the attention I otherwise don't get from my parents, and two, that this is the same attention that I've been lacking since the turning point of coming to the United States. We also were lucky to keep going with all this, until we came to the thought that manic episodes as such are a response, not so much the illness itself, the whole point being to prepare and safeguard against what it is that sets me off. It was a great session.

Money is still definitely an issue for me. When I feel I owe somebody money, mostly my mother, I get a helpless feeling. As if I'm a bottomless pit, as if I'll never be able to make it up. I'm not asked to make it up, as such, but I am held responsible for it to some degree, like when at one of the sessions with Dr.P., mom blurted out that of course those being lent to, hate those who lend or give because that's just the way it is, and I have to wonder now if that's how she felt when everything was taken away from her family and she and the rest of them had not to beg but to ask and to be lent to. In any case this applied to me, as the one receiving.

Yesterday she insisted on giving me a hundred dollars out of two hundred dollars she had as a profit from Atlantic City. This meant many things, to me. Not the least of which that she was grateful for my spending the day with dad while she was gone. But also that she was making me an accomplice, and that once again she was making me an offer I couldn't refuse, since I'm so broke. So, once again in debt to her, a little more.

Yesterday she once again had the caged-in feel about her. Loud, argumentative, dismissive. As I was leaving for Ocean Grove she told me she would have loved to go to the pool but didn't because dad said he wasn't feeling well, so it was decided that neither one would go. Which makes me think she's built this cage on her own, much as I've built my own cage.

I do have a cage of my own. Most people do. Mine has to do with this insistence on returning to the issue of needing attention from my parents, attention they weren't able to give then and are only minimally able to give now. This is my cycle of mania. Over and over again, returning to the same thing, like a riddle I can't solve. Not being able to let it go.

Part of it is my mother's insistence, over time, that she's not needed anymore, when we were going to finish school, and at intervals. There must be a relationship there. Somehow I fell for it every time and wanted to make her feel necessary, in a perverse way. I have to get out of the habit of that.

Last week she went on about dreams she'd had of Nonna and her aunt which in Romanian folklore mean the dead are calling the living to join them, and I fell for it again, for a couple of days. Mother the martyr preparing to die after a thankless existence. Now with this clear day without the Risperdal I realize it's just another martyr-like plea for attention. She doesn't want to die. She's afraid of dying. She's just playing with the idea, as she has before. Which makes me angry, and I have to let it go right away and see how sad it is, this form of getting attention.

Usually I get mad and the road starts to mania. After all I've put into the relationship, all I get is this need on her part to escape, again the martyr. She wants to leave it all behind, responsibility, my father, me. This less than perfect life. She is jealous of my manic flings. She wants some. This is what all this gambling is about - tunnel vision of escape. And I, what do I escape from? From depression for one, over lack of money, over loneliness, over longing for love and friendship. But I also escape from this infuriating farce of martyr and tyrant, control freaks both.

        I am still angry with my parents for carrying this relationship into the "new world," and for letting it intensify to such a degree. I'm still angry at my mother for making my father the villain so that she could be right. She flourished here, he didn't, and she's held the reigns ever since. And yet, the martyr. I find it hard to feel sorry for that. I have to dig a little deeper and look at her youth, at her lack of self-confidence. But in the here and now, what happens is that as soon as I feel better, as I did this week, she goes from being comforting to being almost combative, as if she always wanted to be but was just being nice because I was down. No wonder I want, perversely, to be down, and dependent. It's the only way I get love. Not tough love or rough love but love. When anger rises and I become independent again I have already started on my way to another manic episode, distant or not.

My mother has let herself go. It's not something sudden and maybe she's been breaking down for a long time, maybe because of my father, maybe not. Trying to understand this manic depression has a lot to do with understanding what my mother is all about and I don't know how to put it nicely. I think she let herself go.

It seems to me that in Romania my mother had more of a sense of quality, but maybe that was just because there was so little available that when a person had something it was something of quality or not at all. I was glad for my mother last night when she brought herself that beautiful skirt but I was sad for her too because she never does it on her own initiative.

I know when I go over to their house I'll be frustrated. Mostly I keep quiet. I want to enjoy their company. I know that things will change over time and I'll miss this. I keep returning to this because I think it's important somehow - there is some point to the idea of not letting oneself go. It seems to me there is a quiet agreement among the people who would not let themselves go, that it's worth it. That it's important. That it's beneficial to one's spiritual aspect also.

Maybe people just take care of themselves; maybe they don't have this other aspect in their lives but maybe I'm right. An old friend of the family for example - she's eighty and all this time she hasn't let herself go. Other friends. I don't let myself go. Even in my manic times, even in my most depressed times, it seems to me that it's important not to let oneself go. And I don't mean physically. I mean in the way one acts most of all.

My mother makes it sounds as if everybody who has let themselves go physically has fallen apart in every sense. For these somehow that's implied. That implication is important because I've had the same bias for many years since I was brought up with it. This can't be helped in a normal sense but I can help it by unlearning my behaviour. I can learn to stop criticizing everybody and everything just by scanning their dress or their body. However I'm aware, now that I spend so much time with my parents, that it's an obsession with them: who's fat, who's not; who looks like they have an ailment, and so forth. It seems a very limited way to be, and it is.

I feel responsible for my father, since he has always put me in that position. He would have that go on even now, he would have that go on indefinitely. There are sexual allusions, always those - the one with the other - that I should take care of his physical needs too. No wonder I've tried so hard with my men, no wonder I've needed the elevated connections with certain men as breaths of fresh air. I am so afraid to be touched lovingly, as if I might burn or melt. Someone will have to take me by the hand.

I am a leader, not a follower, but I am not as strong as others. I need help. I am constantly asking for help, or asking for readiness in case I need help. I feel vulnerable now not having someone to long for, to depend on. I am going through withdrawal, after seven years "with" my therapist, a few months "with" a new friend, both of which turned out to be infatuations on my part. I feel open, even cheated, but in the end I am just lonely and afraid.

There is the sense of danger. Books become keys, tokens; I don't know what I'm doing, forging ahead; is it safe to? Probably not, but someone's got to do it. I am sane, all the levels are right, I sleep ten hours most nights, I am becoming more and more spontaneous.

The amount of thought and feeling that goes through me in one day is many times greater than average. I am that spy out in the cold. I have made myself into that, rather than be touched. Yet I would be more.

Today I had to stop myself several times from giving in to great feelings of insecurity. But I dared, and I hung on to myself. I am so proud, I am praying so hard, like the beaten child that I am. No one would or could buy me out. I have to release myself for it to work. If only my parents hadn't treated me like a servant, an indentured one at that.

There is a hardness about both my parents, a willingness to take, take, take. I am callous, but it will have to do. It all has to be casual, in speech, in action, with the awareness of mania but none of its symptoms. Self-control. It gets easier, but the load, the degree, increases. I am amazed that any of it can work, but it does. My life moves forward. I keep wanting to go into a deep sleep and stay, but it is important not to.

Is fear something learned? It is, naturally. Is disquiet a reflex? That is the better question. That sense of being ill at ease, with something, or someone. That isn't fear. When I was waiting to be born, for two days, after the water broke I breathed shallow down the umbilical chord. When I look at myself then, I question everything. I want to know but my wakefulness stops me. When I make knowing, deliberate forays, shields crop up sky high.

It is as though I am kept away. I want to be the same patient, knowing self that I was at the beginning, as I was breathing shallow, and most likely felt exactly this - disquiet. I was hanging in there. I waited. I hung on to life. Whenever I stop to, now, my surroundings won't allow it. Yet.

"There comes a point when we stop living and start just existing." - from The Innocent. That may be, but when occasional whiffs of fresh air remember to hit, we step out again and live and breathe, and stay until someone pulls us back, or some thing. But every time we try harder and harder to stay. Then we go back to the things we do, and in the meantime try to figure it out, to prepare, to remember better how it was to breathe free, to find the way back and out again, to ignore the pain. Not to slip through nostalgia into half-life, that low-maintenance familiar trap. That frightens me more than the pain, and the fear lingers. When it does go I hope I'll be wide awake.

There was a time when I dared plant seeds in the soil; such an action involves hope, although I was void of it at the time. And yet I lived for them, if not for myself. I reminded myself that I have an identity, an apartment, a job, friends, and, finally, someone to guide me through the tremendous pain I couldn't hold off. Only ten years after being told that I need to adjust into the invalid status presented to me, a compassionate soul, a psychologist, had the nerve to say no, you're not crazy, in my professional opinion. And, let's figure this out. I'm here to help.

I felt as if for ten years I'd survived like a sleepwalker grasping at the texture of dark hallways; I was so frightened by the light of day that I dared think of it only as something I would watch again on a screen.

The need to be accepted is so great that I am surrendering my weapons. I can't even say that I don't know what to do, because I do know - exist. This is the most difficult passage, from what was expected of me to what really is, but as much as I feel stripped of all protective layers now, I know that my instinct to persist will not leave me. I am sane. With my doctor's help, I might survive. But I am really here now; I am mourning so many days during which my hands were tied and my face shoved into the mud for screaming out my pain.

The big revelation for me is that I have to act calmly and not interfere even when I sense a problem, or see a blatant one. The only thing I can do is wait and witness. I'd come across this idea before, but each time set it down again as I hurried to alter another person's life, whether at their own request or not.

This need of mine to make a difference is like a disease. If I don't know the people well enough it's not so bad, as in overhearing a conversation, but the closer I feel to a person, the more I feel the urge to interfere, to offer myself as a refuge.

What makes me feel that refuge is needed? It's often appreciated, sometimes taken advantage of, but not my job. And here I come full circle - in my life it's my father who always asked for more, and still does. I have to get a handle on the fact that I will never please him fully and move on. What makes it bad is that so often I've interfered without being asked. Having the idea that I was right or knowing what was right usually backed me up.

Now I think in terms of the absurdity of right and wrong. That implies living with injustice, sometimes, and not making an issue of it. And it implies knowing that the essentials, whatever they are for me, are what count.

Belief. Such a small word. As I let it sink in the first thing that comes is more discomfort. I believe that it's not up to me to save the world or fix it, and that's uncomfortable because there's guilt, and shame, and helplessness. It seems strange that people survive problems, hurdles, pain, abandon. I have waited to be annihilated, by a fist that has yet to come crashing down on me. What do I do, spared as I am, with so much opportunity for recovery? It hurts. I feel wrong starting to enjoy myself.

Up in Alberta, my dependent state would just turn round and round and round in a cycle of helplessness of sorts. Moments of independence linked up as memories that came and went. These days I'm more careful.

It's as if I'd been swimming underwater for years and am now near the surface. I consciously know the ways of insecurity so well that I could navigate them for the rest of my life. But now there's the option of the air above the surface of the water. The air comes in full expansive gulps. The air and the sky, that holds a sun and a moon and the stars. I want that, I long for that. And love, despite everything.

Tonight I'm thinking about my family and how I must accept it all, laughingly, with tolerance, with perseverance. It's not so much that I feel responsible for all of it, anymore, but there's so much pain surfacing steadily, lately. I am close to tears but can't let them out. I stay strong and go through my day the best I can, feeling one thing most of all - that I can't count on them, I can't unload, I can't open up. If I do, the worries flood in with none of the release. Then I'm pinned by worry, rather than sustained soulfully so I can bear what is to come.

All I've wanted for so long is to be able to rest at ease in somebody's arms - not toys, clothes, or money. And then everything passes, I am letting a vast silent moan slip away from me. Something is opening and I must go through with faith, determination, love, with understanding, with acceptance. And again, with love.

Sometimes I wonder how I turned the corner of that street, or followed the curve in the road, and made it home. I have a modest apartment finally, through the government, on a street that's a block-and-a-half long, in a town bordering on my parents'. I live quietly only because I've learned to behave, and how to behave. That is ongoing.

I use power stored in my muscles to stay still; I use it to pick up pen and paper when I've done my chores and am waiting for the next day to come. I tell myself how the day might be and check the boxes for each step. I propel myself through a day or through lunch.

With too much medication I become depressed, so much so that at times I would have chosen either or. Now, I am decidedly like any addict in recovery. A lifetime of caution and self-discipline lies ahead. The kind of highs people seem to dream of come by allowing for a memory. I am manic all the time to an infinitesimal degree. But I pick up the pen, think "easy does it," and write it down. Not long afterwards another task interferes, thankfully.

Then the night comes, and another set of variables with the new day. Sometimes none of it comes soon enough but I still can't get myself to vacuum the floors. I'm better with the dishes. I've created perimeters, which hold the same dimensions as my former cage.

How is it for another person when the walls dissolve, and it's possible, for the first conscious time, to stand upright in the middle of winter? Does that kind of briskness dissolve a person? I find myself running back to gather up the corners, because, in truth, I am afraid. What does it mean, to be spared with my sanity. I don't know. But I'm getting through one day and then another. Maybe all that's left for me is to continue patiently to make less of the mistakes I used to make. Sometimes I don't even know what I'm doing wrong or if it's wrong. The difficulty of expressing what goes on still surprises me.

I have spent a good part of my life trying to excuse my father. This is far more important than the money and the other issues. I have tried to make him what he isn't, what he never was. I was never special to him, he just recognized my sunny disposition and fed on it, and later he didn't and doesn't appreciate me as a woman, but lusts after me.

My current therapist digs in deep at a rate I'm not used to, meaning fast, but the results are there: I do feel incomplete without a man, I did feel the abandonment, I did feel left out in the cold by my father when he told me that I was just a child, when I had thought that I was always more.

I had been filling in for my mother most of my life. Then, started the searches for the lofty and the diving into the gutter, even though it was a nice gutter most of the time. I felt dirty, unworthy of a real partner. I chose men to look up to who were unreachable or had the sense to see my desperation. My therapist was "the" one among the others. He was entirely safe. Married and my therapist. He knew all my secrets and I assumed they didn't bother him because he never said they did. He was the best of my father.

But I got tired, and wanted someone I could have for my own. I leapt at the slightest sign of attention from a new friend. In my head, he became my new man; I had made the complete separation and the new connection, not knowing that my new friend didn't share my feelings, thinking that he did. A couple of weeks later he wrote - don't wait, just switch - and I was relieved because I was confused as to his silences in certain ways and didn't know how to proceed. But I was out in the cold again, and there I have to stay until I figure it out, though not blindly and in bits and pieces this time.

Refraining from responsibility is what it's all about. I want to have responsibility only for my own life, which is plenty in itself. People see me as calm, mature, at ease, and they want some of it, implying that they have some of their own. A client, for example, came in for a massage one morning, and was willing to unload not only physically but verbally, telling me the woes of her weekend, much like my mother would do. I didn't want to hear it, I didn't want to know, but naturally I was polite, indulging her as little as I could.

Digging into a friend's problems may be alright for most people, without any preparation, but for me it isn't. I'm not alarmist or indulgent in such ways. Or maybe I was just overly sensitive to what this woman's day was like. In any case I didn't want to get wrapped up in it. I want to keep my attention for those I choose.

I like to decide for myself whom I let into my life. It doesn't make sense to me to tell somebody a secret just because they told me their secret. Maybe I never wanted to know, like I didn't want to know about my mother's unhappiness with my father, in my teens. There was an intrusion there then, and it still feels like there's an intrusion there now,

when it happens.
      Maybe I am the last person around who still thinks she should be able to say what fits and what doesn't in their own life, instead of accepting interference as the most natural thing. And I'm not talking about random events here. I am talking about deliberate acts. In other words, I am exerting my right not to like people, or to say, this is the limit to which I'm willing to go.
      It's a right I've never given myself before. Maybe that's where all this turmoil is coming from these past couple of days. I, a person with certain shortcomings, am willing to be the one who withdraws rather than continuing in an uncomfortable situation, because I have faith in the friendships I do have and in the future relationships I will have. It gets pretty simple but it's still pretty tough.

      And still I have to think about what someone said about tolerance. Am I being intolerant? Is that what's really going on? Maybe a little of both. I do know that there are people I love and who love me as I am, which makes me think that it's alright to bring up all these questions and be as concerned as I am. But I am in duality, and in Recovery we say to plan, decide and act when we are in duality, so plan, decide, and act, I will.
      I have to trust that I know my own mind. I needn't be afraid to say that despite my history of mental illness. It just is. Even a person with a mental illness can decide for themselves what is right, and not randomly, but with deep conviction.

      When I have felt alone it has always meant that I was searching for a target for affection, I was in despair. I am alone now for the first time in that I don't imagine that anyone is in love with me, and there is no one to fill that spot. I can understand now why and how people, at least people I would know, are careful with their attentions. It makes sense. I've thrown myself around people's necks enough; the pattern shows. It's alright. It will die down now.

      Part of it must have been about the fear of being left out on the street. I have known so much conditional love. But it passes. Everything passes. I can't blame my parents for my good nature, it just is. I can blame them for trying to be the center of my life, all the time. But there I still can't blame them because it's their nature and no more. I just have to live with the traces.

      I panicked when a friend said to move on. It wasn't exactly a ripping but a slow pull of tissue, to the point of tautness. As ever, I turned by what had become reflex to the nearest friendly face, someone who may care for me romantically or not, but is very supportive, someone with whom I have mutual trust. I leapt from stone to stone to him, and I engaged him in a seductive conversation of sorts. I did, to my credit, stop short. Then I started to write again, filling in gaps.

      The fear is of being found out in the sense of dissent, of

lack of agreement with what is being done to oneself. The abused, I along with others, feel that they have to hide, most of all from themselves, if they can. They can't disclose to outsiders what is being done to them because they have been sullied, and in being sullied they are no longer worthy of much at all.

It could be anyone, not just someone with a mental illness, certainly not just an adult. It can be visceral or cerebral or both. Animals have it too. It is instinctual. But once the damage is done there is the need for secrecy, even from oneself. That is how it begins.

In the day hours everything is there to hold the truth down - meals, playgrounds or work, coffee, alcohol. But there are moments in between, slivers of experience, and then the moments at night during which a lack of ease presents itself, so old that it is unidentifiable, not to be grasped at, not to be convinced into oblivion.

There is always the subtext, there is always the implied fear, which I can laugh away, with awareness being so important. It is easy to understand: a family can eat its young, even at Easter or Christmas. A father can make advances and threats to his daughter for over twenty-five years and feel entitled to it. It goes that way. A sister can enter useless frenzies of manic behaviour and be excused as energetic, when I would be hospitalised. A mother is willing to jeopardize my mental health with the threat of withdrawal of funds.

These things add up, but in the morning, as with most families, it is as if none of it had ever happened. The sun is shining, the three-year-old plays sullenly in the living room, trying to get some attention out of her mother, the grandfather comes down like a meek lamb, for now, for his breakfast which is all laid out for him. He likes to be waited on, to be watched, to be spoken to. Who doesn't? I am tired, but I slept at home, and will from now on God-willing while my mother's convalescence unfolds.

The push comes again, and again. How far can I go. How much weight can settle over me? Instantly, I have one child and one child-like father to share with my sister while my mother has a respite of sorts during her recovery from the operation. None of it was necessary, but things were set in motion early, even before I was born. I'm just wading through the molasses until the time will come, soon now, to let go of what has been.

I am only a little restless now. Mostly I'm tired, most of all physically. But I will sleep at home tonight after two nights away, and Friday I'm going out. Meanwhile Orwell's world is filling in the blanks of my life. It feels good not to be hanging on to the thought of any one man, but to enjoy company and thoughts of potential caresses.

I am certain that I will make it through this with my

family. All of it will come together very soon. It will be nice to have my own money and break that spell permanently. More than that, there is bound to be the release.

4.

In this bed, on the night before I flew to Romania last November, Tyler put on his glasses and read my life since my father's passing. We will have to change the sheets soon, fragrant with the sweat of our bodies. Time has passed. The best has happened and has yet to happen, both; love has found a way.

At the counter, the woman with the rotting teeth and bleached layer of hair asked me kindly if I wanted something to eat too. I said "No, just Pepsi." We sat, Tyler and I and another man, a regular. She began her Zen exercise of American cheese slice separation. Another woman came in and began to chat. She was a regular too. The other regular then left by the back door. The burger cook sat down to play an electronic game.
The waitress took a break smoking in the inner chamber, presumably the fridge. She had just gotten off the phone, saying "Stop beating up your younger brother!" I laughed, stopped myself, apologized to Tyler. He said it was okay. It wasn't yet four o'clock and we were all not working in an office.

Often, Tyler will tell me about his deep sorrow, and I will always listen. Love is there for that, and the depth of our love together allows for the repetition that leads to relief on both sides, possibly to absolution.
Yesterday I sat next to Tyler as he prepared for his swim. I watched the sun on the walls of the indoor pool as we talked. I had taken my shower, and being too weak to swim again today I undid my sweater zipper to show Tyler my red silk corset, with my back to the guard. I zipped up again, but he zipped it down and up again.

We sat, lovingly, and now he pulls through stroke after stroke, swimming for both of us. I am barely here, observing from the safety of my body, faintly hoping for good news of work in two days.

At home, I wanted to cover myself with the World Traveler blanket on the couch, to have my sense of waste covered in my weakness, but Tyler drew me out. The day will pass quietly without consequence, other than noticing other people who are not in the golden circle. Maybe this peace of mind, tentative as it is, the recovery stage after more tense moments with my mother yesterday, is the passage to the state of mind I seek, that of acceptance.

Not having achieved anything in the worldly sense, not having the certainty of work in the way of a job in the future, I am faced with the same question: whose standards am I living by, and does everything eventually have to turn into coin to be valid. The kind of poverty some live with every day is crippling, but it is not my poverty. I have run, I have scurried sometimes, I have retreated. I may never be heard but by a limited few, but will it or not I am free of the barriers that hold in the conscious of the every day.

Tyler says the beginning, the being in love part, is the best part. I don't know the rest of it, I don't know anything beyond that. I'm likely never to grow up. Did I mean, mature? Hard to tell. Is that alienation that Alan Watts talks about present in me only part of the time, less than in most? It could be. Do I always reach and long for the state of oneness, or wholeness, of belonging? Most definitely. Do I look for it in others? Yes, I still do that. That is the one thing that will have to change.

It's not just the approval, it's the search for the core, for the essence of my own being through the experience of others. I am always looking, ready to learn, to take in what is freely given, sometimes even what is neglected or discarded. I look for Quality, like Persig and all he spoke for in his work. In searching I am separate from it, but less so all the time. I become part of it. I am relaxing into being.

The woman at the diner is a spent, beaten woman early in her life still, but she shows up and is there, mustering compassion without spite or self-consciousness. She just is, like an aged milkmaid of former days. She pushes her life forward. Today I sit on the bleachers. My space, my line of vision is populated by water cordoned off into lanes, with its most precious cargo, Tyler, making his way through the day's meditation.

I am not removed from him. I have known the water too, though not as a championship swimmer. I know the water now, its meditative longing for the lap swimmer. It is there for one to become one with. Resisting, yet inviting, necessary. In water, lap after lap, there is the experience of having moved through events, and looking forward to making dinner, in Tyler's case, often. In mine is the hope of healing my shoulder before I can return to work healing others.

I notice the woman and let her go. Tyler takes me in as the pretty woman that I am. Why has it always been so painful to allow for something so simple? In the end, can I just be pretty in my new hat and corset? Why do I envy the stability of the woman at the diner? The unknown holds so much, and envy is so short-lived that it is more a recognition of that woman's validity as a human being. But what of my own stability? I flow with my life, fighting to feel worthy of such a day as this, when allowances are made.

Dark is settling, Tyler has come out of the pool while I was looking down at my pad but his black bag is still on the bleachers by the sauna, so I know he is there. In this way another day goes, with a great sense of vulnerability. Another day will be different. I am still trying out the safety that has been created for me so lovingly. Miracles may happen with this gentle thawing out. We will go into the night.

There was the reality of my split heel, in the beginning of October. My mother was still away in Europe. I had been to the basement of the library to stock shelves for the sale, I had seen Tyler there, he had told me not to worry so much about exact grouping of books under sections. We had parted well. I swam, then the door cut my heel open. I ended up skipping out to the office and later the Greulichs picked me up from the hospital where I got stitched up. That stopped the acting classes and 'extra' work.

I am sitting in the bleachers at the pool again while Tyler swims, weak from natural pain, resting today though wanting to be near, in sight of our friends here. I am too tired to fight my life today; in embracing it, I find new strength.

Eight years ago the hopelessness of returning to New Jersey was flooring. I had little to live for then; I have so much to live for now. I have done what needed doing, consistently. Now there is joy, not only in the drowsy sharing of long nights' thoughts and feelings, but also in the anticipation of the melting of old restrictive seams, even of experience.

The personality appraisal chart shows me as "having 'self-power' awareness," living in an introspective reality, focusing on possibilities, using thinking in the form of empirical logic, and "preferring that events and people serve some positive use." "Decisions come naturally...once a decision is made, [I am] at rest." I look to the future rather than to the past.

I am "a builder of systems and the applier of theoretical models," am a "supreme pragmatist," seeing reality as something which is quite arbitrary and made up, and can be used as a tool or ignored. No idea is too far-fetched to be entertained. I'm "a natural brainstormer, always open to new concepts and, in fact, aggressively seeking them, at times very single-minded, in need of both thinking and intuition."

This all came up at the grieving seminar in October, when I was grieving my father's death. Support systems used to matter cerebrally, as I made my way to wellness, and still do, persistently. Now I know what it is to truly have support. In this house, Tyler's and my home, his love fills me, heals me, leads me further into myself while also leading me into the future. I leave behind sheet after sheet of what used to be material, clothing me in pain. There is hope for the future in all ways now. Even the uncertainty of economic instability is diminishing, such a weight in the past, and there is hope of meaningful work as a basis for inner strength. Now is the time for more memories to be made, so that I can let go of even more.

I buried my father alone. When I told Tyler the story, of my sitting there with the box my father was left in on my lap, Tyler said he would have wanted to be there with me. I will not have to do things alone again. I am protected, I am loved, and I no longer have to carry my father. My suffering in that respect has dwindled, wrenched from its foundation by Tyler's vigilant love and compassion. I couldn't have dreamed such love, such healing possible, had it not pulled me in as it has, were it not for the constant reminder of Tyler's flesh, his words, his thoughts.

Pain is cathartic now, where it used to be draining, no more. The loneliness has gone, what was numbness has been penetrated, helplessness is no longer debilitating when it comes. Anxieties are borne better.

"It" continues now as I work, as we swim together in the same lane when I am able to swim. Life continues into health. Growth is both exponential and experiential. I am bound by the tiredness from hours at work, but released from the separation of trying to belong.

I know now that I will not belong with some, while easily falling into a groove with others. There is no discrepancy there, no need for excuses, no fear, though old habits die hard. The "hard sell" can apply to my life as it can apply to work. There is no reason to bend to weakness of character, but there is every reason to accept its reality, its place, even its force of balance to all that is straight and narrow.

I like my discipline, my way back from excursions into the higher elevations of the mind. I need rules, I need to slow down, Recovery-style and listen to the words spoken to and reacted to around me as I come down, as if they matter, because they do.

Make-up bought in the middle of the night from a TV infomercial, for example, too much of it and the excess sold to another, some girl downstairs. I bought my make-up for more that thirty dollars a kit, but does it matter? Of course not. The kit is of value, and it works for her face. Who needs know more. I am surrounded by details of people's lives, and I must tend to them as they reveal truths about their origins.

Another book sale at the library brings us back to how we first spoke together. A young boy looking for his mother has the set facial expression of a doubtful man in his fifties. People buying books mill along shelves like so many ships adrift. Tyler collects their money, I gather myself in written word for the first time in months. It is summer. I wear my string sandals so as not to feel the rub of the other shoes on my bare skin. My heel is still not well after more than eight months. I move on.

I am left helpless in my love for Ioana. Tyler and I are more than well, we are solid together, growing more so each day. Meanwhile my cousin Ioana, the sister I discovered on this last trip to Romania, is so far away. I miss her, would talk to her in person daily if I could. Would walk into her apartment, into her car for a ride, for awhile. Being in Bucharest, she is so far away, despite our frequent talks on the phone. I was looking for her on the other side of the ocean, that first weekend at Asbury Park.

I long for Nicole too, my niece who is now four, knowing there is little I can do. Razvan, Ioana's brother, and his family took me in too, last fall. So I am pinned down by nostalgia, irrefutable and so real, in the midst of my happiness with Tyler. It is as it should be.

Days at the shore bring back memories of childhood, all the hot sand burning our feet, sand thrown down the body of the cement slide to ease the burn. I am not thrown into life as I used to be then; I finally have my own pace, I get to say what happens. I didn't then.

Now I am left with the frustration of accepting my life for what it is, with all the injustice and discomfort of both present and past. If money were no object I would be painting, but it is. So I work, I write, and take joy in Tyler most of all. Things are thrown in my path, I slow down, I even prepare for the foreseeable tough stretches. I have yet to understand why it had to take so long.

At a base level I understand it is all about learning how to get along, that there is always fine tuning to be done. But sometimes hormones don't allow for patience, and I am forced to choose between acceptance and frustration. Some of the time I can bend.

Emancipation, though a word ringing of something new as all freedom is new, is an old word, worn, inherited, lived. I am free in my sorrow even, through tears even when they come, my own and Tyler's. The day I thought they would call about the job I wore my skirt well into the afternoon, nails trimmed, business-like, full of anticipation, and the call failed to come. In the late afternoon, as I said almost to myself, "I guess I can take my skirt off now," something broke in me again, as it had in the past.

What was different was that Tyler followed me into the quiet of the bathroom, so fully understanding my failed hopes for the day that I finally came to know what it is for love to reach across directly between souls of lovers; never had I known such joint pain, so sweetly softened by attention, and affection. I will not feel alone again. Now that I do work, that moment has become so much more important.

The question of my madness diminishes. Tyler is willing to help me see all there is of me, not just the cautionary tale that I have convinced myself of. He populates my mind with thoughts of sturdiness, strength, and even vulnerability without loss. Having shown some of myself to others, I will look inward now, with Tyler's help, and face myself. I am steady in my gaze, even in introspection. The scars, the remains, the housing of my soul, being my body and mind, are whole, but bent, formerly wounded, straightened back into shape to hold, most of all reinforced with the practices of love. Waves of exhaustion and headaches come, but I have the "no-lose attitude," the down side always having merits. Something has been freed in me, in that I find all I need as a base in this house, grounded as it is in the attention to the real, filled with love.

I will no longer erase my own past. I feel safe; I dare clothe myself in my own flesh as I clothe myself in the sweaters and jewelry Tyler gives me, and thus I show up in the world. I am in the haven I wanted and needed so badly, of his heart. I look after myself now, some after Tyler, less after my mother. Things are in place. I stand tall in my new life. The last of the flight from pain is thinning, even if some of it may linger for life.

It, the beginning of the pain, is marked by the return from my trip to Romania, finally stepping onto the Cranford platform at 1:22 in the morning. I waved. Tyler took me home. I hadn't slept, but I had hardened my will enough to make it, and finally I was there. Months later, I am no longer in the apartment to which I used to run. Patty's quilt covers me, warms me, as do all aspects of Tyler's past. My insecurities have flown with the show of love which is unmistakable, coming freely, encompassing all realms of experience. I ache and my joints are tight, my head throbs, and yet my hand moves across the page in pure joy of expression.

The starkness of having outrun my surroundings is gone. I no longer find myself in the brittle light. Matter is clothed in objects that have meaning, many of which have special importance through inherent quality or through association, like so many golden apples strewn everywhere. I will not ask to be turned into a tree like in the myth. I will ask to be allowed to stay, I will even ask kindly to be tamed, harvested, even helped along in the finding of my own voice. This is what will happen in my life now, with pain still brushed loosely in places, a reminder of passages of time, celebrating the resilience of body and spirit. I will go gently now.

For the last time of the cold season, a white hot chocolate at the pool on the bench waiting for Tyler. I took a long time today getting ready. It feels good to sustain clarity, sanity. The thread hasn't broken since before Romania, thanks to Tyler. He has both his feet on the ground, he shows me that he loves me. Tonight we will walk into town for pizza, then watch the country in ruins on TV. I forget about that part enough to keep pleasant thoughts going, to keep doing good things. Without ignoring reality, I am well. My flamboyance and waste of the old days have stopped.

I like it now as things are. What a relief, what a joy. I will watch my surroundings for the rest of my life knowing that it is not always appropriate to lay hands on others so as to soothe them, if only for awhile.

      The trip to Romania was a dream compared to life now. The essence of my relationships with my family there is preserved and reinforced weekly, but I am not likely to visit again for some time. Times are tough, I'm working, and Ireland comes first. There will be a trip next year.

      These days I wait less and less. That's why this afternoon was an exception, but I did well. The waiting was for my mother getting an eye exam. I do not pity her. One day I will have relief. For now she is continually antagonistic and I am tired of being her sponge. If I didn't know better I'd say that it looks like she really can't help herself. It is by choice though. My mother chooses to impose on from big to small, and she is ready with resentment before any task is even completed.

      I used to think it was my fault, because she would have me believe it. But the sting is not as strong these days, not as deep. In time, maybe a short time from now, I may be able to do without her financial help for good. A little at a time, I will get there. Steady now is the only approach. For now she still provokes me, creating opportunities to do so, tries to exert her power over me. She is "dynamic outer environment" indeed.

      Tyler is a world of support and my source of love and constant understanding. With his help I will not revert to old habits. My love for him grows, in no small way because I see how well he does in having patience with me. He understands and accepts our limited time together; he is all I want and need. He has risen to the occasion with more wisdom, love and patience than I ever would have thought possible.

      It makes it so much easier to bear my mother, having him as a mate, often my guide, my lover, my friend. When I go home tonight, it will be to him, not to an empty apartment or a spiteful parent. It is a delicate balance to keep and it is love that allows for it. I have never known anything like this love and acceptance, with my own need to smell his skin and kiss his lips, touch his bare body when we can. CookieO'Puss loves it all too. I've never seen her so happy. I can pull all the stops now.

They are telling us that the loading crane is stuck in the cargo door of the plane. I am tired, aware that I will not sleep for twenty-four hours or more. I will harden my will. I have come a long way. In Romania, soccer will be on this Sunday night. Real life does not wait for the comfort we are all force-fed in commercials. What it does is allow for little thresholds, little check points to refer to later.

I was in the kitchen at 19A Drobeta waiting for Kiki to take in the idea of the Brita filter as a way toward recovery. Extravagant gestures live briefly if at all in such a context. The flow of life we shared that afternoon may be long gone.

I glide through my life aware now that the gestures I give such importance to are not going to survive, though some may never fade altogether. What is essential is that I have done my job, in that I continue to stand by my relationships. I have to be quiet while experiencing pain related to my family, while I thaw out my innards, while I form newly stretched thoughts of love, of becoming a woman. There is nothing artificial, just the occasional pocket of the silence of the unknown.

I wake up in the middle of the activity of the day as such, with these little spaces of the past, with the emptiness of feeling the need to please when I know I already do. It will take some time to know who I am, but it is happening.

I started off my journey with the twenty-dollar bill from my mother at the station and some thirty of my own. I was carrying my leather bag in heavy rush hour, with the backpack and gray flannel bag on my shoulder. There was so much ahead. Tyler's words carried me through Penn Station to the A train to the air train to the KLM terminal. The woman at the counter was as tired as I was. She took both my bags; I went into the waiting area to get some last cash out of the account and waited.

Seven years had passed. Whatever I was doing, it was without fear. The second day, when Mioara took me on foot to the post office, I knew that I had done well to dare. I dare still, to be spontaneous, to move through my life. Tyler's letter said: "your home will always be in America..." He was claiming me. It felt fine. Now my home will always be with him. He is an American, I am too, and we are both citizens of the world besides. We have found each other.

On the last leg of the journey I put the boarding passes and my notes for Tyler together to send off. I was awake with the shot of coffee and the snack. Later I found out from Mioara that they expected both of us, my mother and me, till the last moment when I walked into the waiting area. I had yanked my bag by the handle off the carousel and the handle had come right off. So I put the bag upright, on its wheels, buttoned up, loaded the backpack and went forth. We were to spend three hours in traffic that night, getting to their apartment. I armed myself with a reserve of smiles, and there they were, masking their disappointment well.

The hallway of their building hadn't changed. Same grungy walls, low ceilings, up to the passage leading to the elevators. The stairwell waited unlit on the left. We squeezed into the 'lift' to the six floor, their door being right next to the elevator shaft. At night I could hear the comforting muffled sound of the precise stopping motion of the thing when someone got off on our floor.

I might as well have been born with that sound, like others in time were born with the sound of the rocking chair or the ticking wall clock. I grew up with the sound of the final destination up to Nonna's home at Drobeta. Now the sound came again, irreplaceable.

On opening the door to the apartment I sunk into the old life as I had known it, might have been immersed in it. There was no longer the luxury of the apartment on the fourth floor, but reality now, the small kitchen down the hall, all the coats behind the door, the cabinet with the cloth drawn across where the glass had been, broken so recently that it was mentioned. I sunk or immersed myself into Romanian, borne along by events, into the language of what had been.

But they, Kiki and Mioara, were still in this place, guides out of nostalgia into the tangible. I contributed the pasta salad from the plane, which I hadn't opened, to the one Kiki made for us. Cyril the cat made his appearance, and I was told to leave the doors open to the bathroom for his use. I unloaded my few things. Throughout, they were both able to not show that they had wanted my mother to come, that they thought my trip was the excuse.

I handed Kiki Nonna's passport. They both looked at it. In the picture, at seventy, Nonna looked easily ten years younger. Mioara never got to meet Nonna. Nonna was for Kiki a little like Linda is for Tyler in that she will never be away, always there as a source for comfort. I know and respect that. Mioara has taught me a lot when it comes to that. Some things one must never compare to, some people have fulfilled the ones we love in ways that we cannot, and we must be grateful that the thing or person was there or is there in memory. So with Nonna and Mioara. Mioara, the 'other woman' at the time Nonna came to the States, under scrutiny, who survived the years of humiliation of the separation from the first wife, for the sake of her love for my uncle.

Time passes. The worries of the early morning are gone. After some hours of work, doing my taxes, paying a bill, then a good swim, the chemical insecurity that came with physical discomfort is gone, in the brilliant light of day. With hope, things move forward.

I have to hold out hope that what is disturbing for now during the week is not that important, certainly not essential to the larger task. I will have to fit the job to me, not the other way around. The table before me has withstood fifty years. Aluminum legs, quilted plastic top. Here I sit, after having petted my love gingerly without a clear idea of the effect, other than the love that surrounds us. I have been so broken. Tyler continues to make me whole.

My world is a few drawers, this desk with the writing tools, a few boxes, the dust I have sucked from the floor of the living room and this room. Part of my life is the lack of something, like the lack now of this dust. Have I done right? Yes, decidedly. I have myself, and myself in the warm bed with my love. I have it all, the olive curtains I brought to this room, my things which will trickle in. Tyler has let me in, and things will never be the same.

I will accept the silence as to my past as a valid wish. None of it matters anyway. What there was before was not love but stunted effort. That is alright, it has to be alright and it is. So little compared to so much promise of love. There are times when silence is part of the wisdom. The flow of life as it should be has begun, and I am grateful for that.

The sound of the carols in the kitchen at Christmas comforted me. Tyler wrapped me in the Christmas way of things, drastically healing what was left of the wound of uprooting, twenty-eight years before. He only knows part of the effect. I know, though. When my mother has finally found her way elsewhere, maybe next year with my sister, the last of my irritated nerve endings will let go of the last of the pain.

Tyler's world is waiting to pour into me and I can be the vessel to hold it. I too have things to say and memories to record in ways that will last. The point of departure to the real is being constantly reinvented. If there is death at the end of each completed act of creation, there is death now, exquisitely transferring links to the next level. Meaning, this journey of the recent past begins and ends with every paragraph, and the break of the rhythm is like the break of the flow of breath, with the sense of the emptiness at the moment of complete exhalation of breath. The diaphragm will always intuitively lower again, pulling in breath, even if lungs fall behind. So with this, there is something present in the nothingness.

Time folds over us at the end of the day. It is our first weekend away from home. Everywhere there are signs of the passage of time by the ocean at Asbury. I wake up to the reality that I have been fed lies, mostly, until Tyler. In the brilliant sunshine, as my skin tans, I want to hide, more than under the umbrella. It will take time to unwind from a lifetime of insecurity.

We rode the wild surf, I heading into it, Tyler riding with it. The current was strong, leaving me with a rope burn on my right leg from the lifeguard enclosure line. Then Tyler taught me how to fly my first kite. At the age of forty-one, I am adding a layer of missed childhood to my life.

We loved our room in the afternoon, in the peace of the night. Tyler was drawing out painful untruths like so many needles that need to come out, so that they may be gone forever. My hair is grown, drawing compliments, too. I try not to be overwhelmed by a sense of time lost questioning my own self due to doubts instilled by others. I am entering the life I always wanted.

The little white space beckons. The notepad has become a ritual. This is the third one. One ended up in Trimmings last year, one got partially used in Romania and was left behind there in November, and now this one. I remember the cost of the first one being almost prohibitive when I bought it, the morning I sat in my doctor's waiting room and wrote.

What would life be without impediments. Now the distraction of the radio in the waiting room at Maureen's marks time. Last year at this time I was still seeing Mike. Last year life was forlorn and unbearable, with the prospect of my father's illness dragging on for years. By the time he died I had stopped seeing Mike.

The door to the middle room is locked, when it shouldn't be. Beyond lies the freshly painted wall. There are spirits in this house. Tyler will have to open the door with a knife. Having just come out of the bath, alone in the house at night, I have the feeling of a young child, the little dread that passes through. The Christmas ornament with the picture of the Home Alone kid is next to the candy dish, on the table to my left. My letters from Romania are still there between the foot of the lamp and the candy dish. There, I walked to the post office as if my life depended on it, and in a way it did.

In the locker room, Shirley Basey is singing Killing Me Softly overhead. She sang that thirty years ago on Romanian television. Time gets muddled on the easy-listening station. I will write about traveling, grasping an indefinite nature yet worthwhile. A person can travel from here to the post office or across the ocean. The journey of discovery can lead anywhere.

What happens when a person is torn from their surroundings? Tyler traveled to seek his home as he knew he might experience it someday, free of impositions, knowing only barely that it could happen. Others travel to escape, and are thrown back into the same existence at the end. But something happens to all of us who travel. I wore these jeans, which have shrunk now, to Romania. My ankle is more than exposed. In time I will give them away. I am blissfully well in my own skin.

The car takes us places. I ride often as a passenger now, and I wonder at the passage through space in this rudimentary box, well-cared for though it is. I lose myself a little, tripping by nature when drugs do not overwhelm. I remember days, moments, in other places, in other cars, each moment specific. I wonder how I'm here, having passed through space as much as I have.

Memories merging are related to a sense of loss, so much gossamer having passed through my fingers. Now there is little I can do but witness. I feel the pain of loss implied in a new beginning. The past is torn away and I remain standing, with so much help, to pick up my broken self.

The day after the fourth of July, after more rain, Tyler drifts with his eyes closed next to me at the arts center before the show. People are impersonating Elvis. A subculture overcomes the economy tonight. People come out in numbers to feed on a dream. The street is still wet when we leave but we have seen people live, having dusted off corners of their mind for a couple of hours. We have lived too, creating new corners to seek refuge in, in turn.

I know so little, but I am reassured that in time I will know more. After the trip to Romania, there is the rest of my life. In the essence of things there is love, the experience of it, the anticipation, the desire. It flows through us, neatly. Life is full of wonder. It happens. We run with it. I am getting out of the way of love, so that it will more comfortably settle in of its own.

Lost of all things in a reverie of love, so much a sweet thing, I am brought back by people who know little of what goes on, who wish me well in the way of caution. I am tired of my fate in this respect. Tyler looks after me, I do what I can for him. He is my lover, my love. I feel melancholy today at the thought of so much loneliness these past twenty-five years. Enough is enough.

My insecurities fly from post to post during the day, and although with time they are likely to lessen, the process drags on. As patterns shift and new patterns form, old patterns fade. There is no set rule. Communication is key, still. So is awareness, and a willingness to pay attention to the same. I have been on my own for so long that in the car with Tyler sometimes I realize that my meditations are abstract. Thoughts often do not gel into words. I do what I can not to force words out of my mouth when they would not come. I am teeming with sensations, yet they do not find their way to a threshold of expression. Interestingly this is not the drugged-out experience. It is the sense of being unable to communicate at a time when a lot of adjustments are being made. When words do come, the thoughts are new.

Misunderstandings tear their way through life, as they always will; there is the sense of needing to work carefully through them. Hurdles have come in a row and they have only now begun to turn into positive obstacles. Love is there, as much as there is ever likely to be love. The silences weigh heavy. We have to bear them until the wave of release comes. Concepts, foreign to real experience, impose themselves out of habit, though we are not of the ordinary. With that in mind we will be well. There is just more to pass through and we will pass through it. We are not entirely separate anymore, nor are we likely to be that again. There will be no games.

I grow up unexpectedly, with less insecurity. I have myself now, and it has so much to do with him. There is nothing to lose in loving and living fully from now on. To be spontaneous is most important of all. My body tires. I recover and redouble my efforts. If it weren't for

Tyler I might slide back into the dream of depression which has been my life. Early on it was melancholy, even sweet melancholy, but for such a long time it has been something else. Something was broken in me. Now I live.

   The pain of the past comes rushing into our lives anyway, the choppiness of the world persists. I would love to clothe Tyler into a blanket of rest, one like the blanket that covers him now on the couch. The pain of the past rests in his bones, as it does in mine. I have seen ahead to some time from now when the oppression of the past will have melted away. There are things of the real, such as this notebook, given so lovingly. I have hung on to such few things.

   The radio reminds me that there are people in the world other than the two of us. I need to be mindful of the fact that Tyler is made up of details, as well as a whole. My details do not settle as much. I have been busy pushing my details into the future that there is only the constant flow. It used to be that the constant flow came from fear, the motion being perpetual so that the past would not catch up. Part of my need to communicate has been about this pushing what is now, into the future.

   Can I stand still? I can at times, often enough now. I am willing, ready and able. Tyler is my guide. I put my faith in him. This year I have gathered the strength to dare as I have never dared before. If that makes me a little rough, it will have to do. I am myself wherever I go now.

   Life is forever the making and unmaking of details. It comes so clearly to me this morning, at eight-thirty in the laundromat. Getting up and doing what I said I would do was all that needed to happen. Later Maureen and I will talk about my sensitivity regarding money. It is important to deal with this, all the duality that needs tackling. Did I protest my independence too much yesterday? For me, clean laundry brings with it thoughts of absolution. If I can get it all washed, dried, and put away, everything is in its place and will be well.

   My shifting patterns, with insecurities in tow, mean growth. So the building and undoing of details, checking on familiar faces, doing the rounds of what stands as familiar. My need to regurgitate experience becomes apparent. Doing that is part of the process. A version of Who's Afraid of Virginia Woolf is the last thing I want in my life, but that's what happened last night. I'm sorry for my own sake, and for both of us.

   As the laundry is drying, details fill the room. This notebook, given so lovingly to fill, the scarred face of the attendant with the curly blond hair, the Las Vegas plastic bag of the man with the bulldog face. Outside, cars pass. Damage is done. Can damage be undone just as easily? Sitting in the living room next to Tyler now, I pay attention without disrupting, hoping for the best.

This may be the last night of the Christmas tree. Time has moved us forward. The fire pops, and again, in the fireplace. We watch death over and over again on TV. I have been eating so much meat, mostly remembering to pray for forgiveness, enjoying what I used to deny myself. It has been some time that I've been saying Grace before meals, in silence. It seems fitting.

I learn so much every day in my life with Tyler, in the life we are making for each other. We are both developing as human beings, separately and together. We are living the every-day, becoming fulfilled. If it takes medication, alcohol, coffee, or cigarettes, there is no wrong way to get there. The point is to be on the way. It's alright if progress is partial or intermittent. There's the hope that in time it will become a permanent state of being.

Whatever gets us there is alright with me, to that clarity which would come with fasting and the like, too. The body is depleted or overwhelmed either way. There is no wrong or right way, just so that the object is reached.

To me, the mess we live in as people IS perfection. There never was a better time. That is an illusion. There will never be a better time. The perfection lies between the drops. Moments of perfection happen all the time. Some we manufacture, some we look forward to and they never come. Some we enter knowingly, some we can even stretch and recall.

The Scottish bar was one of those moments of perfection, Tyler bringing us there and sitting us down, the time as it slid by us past the postcards and the beer and the ginger ale, the Scotch for Jim McIntyre and the Irish coffee. We faced the bar, we walked down the stairs. I never want to be there without him. I know the place through the thought of Tyler. Around us, people came and went, some watched; we did not watch them in return. It was natural that they were there, that the room was full, that the boys behind the bar made the drinks and poured the beer. It was all for us. Everything helps me forward.

There's the act of traveling, then there's memory, and then there's the imagining of what might be. In movies, things are evoked: we may be able to relate but not fully know. Movies, books, stories, are invitations to travel. For now, I will stay with the real. There's plenty in that. There are the journeys of the everyday, to the store, the pool. Then there's more.

I remember now the journeys on our bikes when I was little, which have now become one. My father would get us ready and off we'd go to climb trees in the parking lots of the hotels by the sea, the deserted village of Mamaia. One day my cat, whom we'd packed in a basket, climbed too high a branch. It was just something that happened, but it became a marker, something to be remembered as unusual. Now I have something to hold on to from that time.

It took time to get there, to those parking lots. We always grew tired enough to turn back. Something happened. Toil went into those trips. My father had taught us how to ride, and to swim. Grooves had been worn into the flat pattern of our lives, of our common experience. The act of biking left traces each time, in the muscle fibers. As my body shapes up now, with all the swimming, I tone the same muscles which once walked and biked those roads. There is dormant history there.

I will take this journey where it takes me, gathering memories and momentum, and I will let things air out along the way. I trust that I am a traveler, and that there are reasons for me to express what I have seen, what I know.

There is movement in my life, much like in a piece of music. Tyler says the nicest things. I will leave the heaviness in with the rest, for measure. The waves are real, but worries fade in time. In the heat of summer, I still push through my life to something better. A burger waits for me at home, yet to be cooked tenderly by my love.

Will this be my time? I have begun and stuttered so many times, in so many ways. I write in the morning, eager to put together my new life in words. The day comes with work and frustrations of incomplete interaction there. Then the ride home in the car, older now despite new spark plugs and belt. I long to know myself as Tyler sees me, full of goodness.

The jeans splashed with bleach will no longer leave home. I'll use them for painting. The brand new velour pants have a clean slate while these shrunken jeans, washed so many times over, came to Europe with me the past few years. They were my shield from the elements, as well as from the environment I found myself in. They allowed me to function, as clothes do in the best of cases, without being too aware of myself.

Many years ago I went to Salt Lake City in clothes I no longer have, and flew back shortly after midnight. There were flowing layers of gauze over the seamless tights I'd held on to from Canada. I arrived as a sign of spring in February, while snow still covered the cottages of Sundance Village at the end of the cab ride. The festival had come and gone, the Olympics were over, and I was there to mark the spot in a flight of folly that was the result of my anger towards my mother.

I stayed only hours, called for a cab and a plane ticket from the gift shop with some help, drove to the airport on the night road and boarded a packed flight back to JFK. The people around me were intent on their journeying. I sat planning to get a ride back to Newark Airport, where I'd started out, to pick up my car and confront my parents, who would talk me into the hospital again. There the doctor said, in the end, when it was clear that the drugs were hardly off the mark at all, that I should have less arguments with my mother.

I had felt compelled to go, in the middle of the night, having printed out an e-ticket for the first flight to Salt Lake. I drove to the airport to wait. When I got there, everything was on low. I talked to a janitor for a while, then I went for a ride down the parkway, came back on a manic high alright, the agent on the job, in pursuit of a goal. It was so easy. I wouldn't do it now, because now I value things and money more, because they no longer seem disposable, as they did at the time. Tyler has brought me to earth.

In a hotel room by the 'sea' I dreamt of a hotel room by the sea, in the afternoon. I have finally caught up for the week. In the dream, there were things moving and towels flying upright around the room. In the dream I told Tyler about it and he said, "Oh, well, that's Asbury Park."

I woke up, had some corn chips and came back under the umbrella. It is enough to be surrounded by the sound, sight and smell of the ocean today, Tyler and all the people. He was looking for me when I got here, I missed him on waking up and came looking for him.

On the second day of the weekend, still under the umbrella, I am wide awake and well. I had hoped to be this well today. In the end, so much is about maintenance. Food, drink, sleep, a hot bath. By now I know the signs of wear. If the basics are satisfied, more can happen. If they aren't, things can happen but at a price.

Tyler's dark skin against the sky-blue towel, lime green of the umbrella, and neon orange of the beach bag, clothes him so well. It is the body's largest organ, the newsletter said. Work is looming, tomorrow.

A long time ago I learned not to take anything for granted. After another Nagle's burger, after ginger ale at the bar at the end of the road, I sit in Tyler's beach chair facing the ocean of early evening. We will see the fireworks here tonight and drive home in the darkness, in the cool breeze. Work will come soon enough. It is this life that needs to come first. There's no need to see too far ahead.

I will leave on time for work, full of unequalled experience. In exponential terms, I have fed on food of the gods this weekend. What has passed through me, and the way that it did, will not be mere diversion; something has changed for good, for the better.

I have sought approval all my life from my family, the only ones who wouldn't give it to me. Tyler, my new family now, other that my cousins who also know how to live, has just fixed the line of the Skull kite. Now he's heading past the Convention Hall with it in tow, way, way up in the sky. I ran along the beach with it to get it started. Far away, some time from now, I will help sail a boat. We just say that things will happen and they do.

Someone has forgotten or left behind a striped white and green sheet on the sand, wet probably like our towels when we got back from our walk. Nothing bothers me. In this little chair, I am happier than a queen. I have been restored. One day we will go to Ireland. One of the things that I love about Tyler is that he will not boast. He had the patience and the desire to allow Ireland to sink into him, and he was able to put what he saw and felt there across to other people in written word. The love of Ireland that he experienced throughout that time, a lost time now, is so evident in his continued longing for it that I wish we could go right away. In time, we will.

I am about to turn the corner into knowing how to relax. I can feel it. The last vanguard reactions insist on their right to continue on, as old patterns will, but they're less likely to win than they used to. I am determined to move forward.

Today, coming home from a morning's work, the timing belt melted. When it fell off, the power steering went, then the air conditioner, bringing on the battery light. Later now at the pool with Tyler it's already decided that it will be in good hands on Monday, so that I can relax and enjoy the weekend. Things can be more simple than they have been.

I am tired of a lifetime of worrying. It's good to fight it consciously now. Maybe I don't always have to be on trial. Tyler loves and accepts me. I need to let that sink in, instead of having the refrain in my mind of "there is something wrong with you." That could get tiresome to even the most loving mate.

He will come out of the pool soon and we will be on our way, to the store for veggies, then home for an evening of burgers and dogs with friends. Life does not have to be a fiasco, even when things go wrong. Here he comes.

"Sanity and insanity are matters of motive, not rationality or competence. The sane are constructive, the insane are destructive." So it says in a business book, making me reconsider everything once again. It borders on use of creativity, if I understand it right. I will be thinking about this for awhile.

A very basic equation is at work in my mind: my happiness depends on my being able to satisfy others. As soon as my love has a blue day or a black afternoon, I feel that I have failed. If friends reject me, the effect is compounded.

Something was taken from me early on, a core of self-assurance, which I have to find again. If I am to get over devastating lows, that has to happen. There is no doubt that I have my father to thank for this, primarily. He demanded my love for a very long time, without apology or excuse. The rest of my family, excluding my cousins, encouraged self-effacing behaviour.

I am trying to make up for being bipolar, still, after all this time. But even before that, I was trying to make up for lacks that were never mine. Cerebrally I know now that my mother stopped loving my father before I was born, and that I tried to fill her place emotionally because my father encouraged it, but in practical terms the knowledge does not bring relief. She continues to harbour resentment toward me, acting as if she has a right to my existence, though Tyler shields me well. In her mind, Tyler wasn't supposed to happen, in her mind I should have become her caretaker, with little life of my own.

In my mind I go the platform I've left so many times, always on the way to New York, never west. I go vaguely to the early morning days more than twenty years ago, packing artwork on busy trains. Then to the late Sunday nights with laundry done at my parents' place, heading home. Those days were laden with worry, the burden of insufficiency, and the sense of being depleted time and again, having to start from scratch. When I stared out into the night, nothing would come back in return. Just passing light after passing light over industrial landscapes, until the walk home down the city streets.

I would try to forget once again what I had known so that there might be room for what I would want myself, not what was spoon-fed. Grooves formed in my memory with those trips till they became one massive path. The trip east now leads me there, into the middle of things, every time into my own core.

The malaise sinks in and lingers, with my mother. There isn't any moment of true ease, of relaxation. Things are evaluated and pulled down or put down. It's hard to take. I feel polluted again, like I used to. She brings me back. Last year I had this feeling about both of them. Tyler wasn't there. Now he is, and only my mother is left. I have to hang in there. It's enough now, but it goes on.

Things have new meaning when they are bought well, especially after an adulthood of squandering. Do I insist too much on the basics? I might have, in the past. Now basics are taken care of, only differently. Tyler's spontaneity is rubbing off and settling in at the same time. He moves so smoothly within his self-appointed limitations, that I cannot help but admire him; I slip into the groove without losing track of myself. Things are good.

Ioana reached across the phone line today and shook me into a level of well-being. Her love steadies me in my purpose, of making myself the center of my own life, not my mother. It is such a simple difficult thing. Ioana is right. God does set things straight. My mother will be in Europe for awhile. With this trip, the last of my transition to my new home will be complete when I bring Josie to our house.

Last year I thought I was doomed to hold things up more because there was the house and my father. With Josie here where she belongs it will be alright for my mother to give up her apartment and move to Europe, if it comes to that. That couch that came in through the window can go out the window again. Things weigh so much, but only for so long.

Tyler's past is alive in him, in the sense that his recall of times and places past is remarkable. I remember things in the way of moods, certainly tainted by circumstances as much as the place witnessed. I already knew that other people remembered things differently, from their descriptions, but most memories had seemed to dull with time. Tyler's are crystal-clear, once awakened.

Looking at slides of his times in Europe is not a pastime, but a journey into being, Tyler's being. To him the places are not memories, even if some no longer exist in the same way. To him the dampness of the grass is still there in the hillside, and he knows just what is around the corner. He fills in experience as he might fill the blank pages of a book with vibrant calligraphy. His eyes have the same steady gaze they had when he was in his thirties, even now. It is thrilling to know this much.

Can it be as simple as airing out enough to find oneself truly among others, not alone? Getting my writing into a finished form last year and having people read it did for me what nothing had done before: I had always known that I was worthwhile as a human being, but until then I had struggled alone for the most part, doing the trick of convincing myself I'm alright every day. I'm still doing that some, even now, but a year ago it was my last and best shot.

Then, the writing made it so that I might reach someone, so that I might be heard. Then I was heard, and some good people came into my life, most of all Tyler. He doesn't need the trick. He knows he is a poet, a photographer, and so much more. But I think now that getting his work seen by more than a few would create that ratio I told him about: more people occupying his mind with positive comments than not, edging out the pain of neglect inflicted in the past.

I am starting to trust in what is. That is the simple part. Tyler's nature is complex. He is infinitely worthy of all the time it may take for things to come out on their own, with some dislodging of pain so old that there must be effort made, time and again. I wait. I used to push. So little and so much will come out, not as things are thought to be. I'm lucky because anything goes, all is beneficial. I have to be true in my humility. I have the gift of certainty of purpose in just being, living for the idea of service.

I return to the thought of work, moving steadily if cautiously and slowly, toward my own independence, which has eluded me for so long. I have dug my head down deep for years hoping it might happen, and now it may. Gently now. It may happen yet. Allan Watts struck home over dinner last night about being part of the present, past and future at the same time. The future is now, every second, and I must live accordingly, openly. It is happening.

5.

The Bowery Ballroom might have been a contradiction of terms, until tonight. Kenmare Street turned into Delancey where it met the Bowery, on the way back from Chinatown and Little Italy. On the last day of November, Tyler and I walked in the rain to get there. The night was our first night together in the city.

We came to know each other from such different directions, albeit in Cranford. In the rain, in the cold, our stride is the same. Tonight will be nice and easy walking up to the hotel. Tonight we won't run for the train, then make it home in the cold to our own bed. CookieO'Puss will wonder, again. This will be our third night away from our home.

I used to do so much to keep my cat happy. With a more balanced life now it is obvious to me that CookieO'Puss will always be a little nervous; some cats just are. It is equally apparent that Ioana is having a hard time and is focusing perhaps disproportionately on her animals. I can assume no more until I see her in person in six weeks. Her essential oils successfully bought, I won't have to come back into the city before we leave. Six weeks of work with Christmas Eve and Christmas, New Year's Eve and New Year's as my days off. Life doesn't ease up much, but Tyler is by my side.

Having soup next door from Dr.Gallina's, I am allowing myself a luxury. It was needed. I am peaceful and very tired, glad to surround myself with daytime pub noises. America is afraid on so many levels. I needed a break. As my love for Tyler grows, I realize that I have to put myself first in my own life, starting now and for good, physically and in other ways. I cannot afford to fall apart.

It's ironic that in a country we as kids in Romania imagined as the lap of luxury, there is so much of a refugee approach. Tyler shares his life with me one antique Christmas ornament at a time. He was never beaten down inwardly, but something was taken from him. And yet so much love pours out from him to me daily. We may be lucky and heal each other yet. There are no guarantees but there is the possibility. That is enough to go on for now. Life unfolds, the more I relax.

On a soupy day near the end of the year, I gather myself. After weeks of continuous work, my body demands attention in its sense of weakness with chest congestion. Yesterday, after making the effort necessary to mail my mother's express package to Switzerland, where she is visiting my sister, I heard her strike her mightiest with the comment: "You'd better hurry up and get well, because you're the one who brings in the money." Her lack of gratitude stays with her.

Near the end of the day, I watch Tyler prepare to swim. The milky fog is deepening with the coming night. We will go look for a dress for Antoaneta after. In three weeks from Monday we will start our trip east to Romania. I will bring my old curtains for Mioara to upholster their chairs with. Kiki would have us not go to Constanta for the sake of what he thinks belongs to my mother.

We came from the library, where I was reminded again of the resources available to us as citizens of this small town. There were no lines at the checkout counter, but the clerk was frazzled. The one I like most wasn't there. We had to narrow our selection to help her, and we did. Tyler cautioned me gently with his hand, not to push. He was right. I have been so used to always needing options and finding alternatives that now, when I am relearning everything, I continue to have the impulse to correct wrongs and injustices, but I can finally let it go as it comes.

By not working because I'm sick this weekend I am 'losing money.' But with the rest, with the slowing down, insights flood. In years to come I will see confirmation of what I feel now: that the money 'lost' has gained me entrance to another stage of my life. My mother's comment was uncalled for and inaccurate, but at least in making it my mother sliced away another layer of the illusion of my dependence on her. In time the struggle will be over and I will have survived it, as I did my father. We all have our own legacy.

Through the massage work I've been doing, I've had it confirmed beyond a doubt that I am gifted to the point of healing. In time more will happen with that. The knowledge of my own strength in this respect is so deep that no amount of demeaning behaviour on behalf of receptionists or even family members will shake the foundation now firmly laid. That was the point of the recent marathon. My body is toned and strong in general, just a little weak for now. I can live with that.

The idea of part-acts, old-fashioned Recovery style, comes up again and again. My heel is not able to stand a regular shoe even now, but this morning I gathered myself and sent a note and pictures to the company that used to get me 'extra' work. There is no reason to rule that out. It is yet another aspect of my life, observing 'life' on stage from the background. I have dismissed my life and my own hard work within it too easily in the past. Not everyone can say they have done what I have. It is time to turn things around into worth, as Tyler has just done, once again, coming out of the pool. With him, I am becoming whole. I have asked for what I need, and it has been granted.

Over Christmas, the Middle East has exploded into a more difficult situation than ever. The weight of the effects has only begun to settle.

I have never felt so much a part of a life together. In the kitchen last night, I had put on my black Christmas dress with the broach he gave me for Christmas. I was beautiful for him as we discussed the remains of democratic ideals in the United States. The world felt small and vulnerable in our kitchen, which is full of life but lacking in glamour. Our little forum went undisturbed after dinner, and I went to bed early, but still this current sickness will have to take its course.

I called Kiki to let him know I won't be able to invite everybody out to dinner before we leave Bucharest, because of the money I didn't earn these four days. I agreed that for once my mother was right, but only because of this time out of work. My mother is setting me free unintentionally by leaps and bounds with this last desperate attempt to put me in my place. Today her credit card bill came, which I will write out one of her checks for, as she asked. In less than a month she has spent a small fortune helping my sister with groceries in Switzerland, but a special dinner for me at a special time in a special place is something that she would not let me have.

Through this small victory she has lost me for good. I will pay her bills, pick her up at the airport, I have even tried today with little success to fix the ill-fated drawers my sister had her buy, the week my father died. But with each act, I will distance myself from any true filial responsibility towards her a little more. After what has been a life-long effort there is only the equivalent of a dustpan of unresolved nagging unworthiness. With that deposited safely in the garbage once and for all, I will be able to walk confidently into the night with Tyler, and be well.

A home such as ours is not a concept. Even the cat, who's hidden so much in the past, knows it. She has free will, sitting by the foot of my chair. The music box plays the theme of the cottage in the movie as we prepare for the New Year. Tyler will cook after all. I have made a fire. The outdoor lights sway in the winter night while I watch a timely Redford movie. Almost out of debt, past hardships behind me, I am ready to consider more.

Around me, so many details come together; things work. The sterno cans are about to be lit for the feast. I am not an innocent. I was worn down, days ago before the bug found its place in my chest and forced this time off work. Now I look up from the pad to the tree, colourful, warm, held in place with rope. Tyler opened the back door and wind blew in. Candles burn. As much as I would share this night with Ioana, I know I can't. She is accomplishing things in her life, acquiring debt as need be, proudly aware of what it will cost her.

Tyler puts out party-time paper plates and napkins. This home is different from any home I have known in that everything has its place, having come to it in time, having settled, yet in constant use and flow. We have tried to document the tree, but it will fade into memory eventually, not to be replicated. The air moving in the room makes the tinsel sway, lightly. Air pockets burst in the fireplace.

When the movie is over, the news will come on, all bad. There will be people freezing in Times Square tonight. No, we will not go out. We didn't last year, either. We are home bodies.

Tyler fell in love with me deeply in the kitchen of my apartment over a year ago, at the sight of my wooden chair austerely facing the small TV on the table. He understood then that that was my life. I had cable then, but it was all I had. I was holding on by a thread. Things have changed alright.

There is no reason to go persistently after changes that may never come. It makes more sense to me to adjust to what is, to stop whenever necessary and reconsider, for the sake of making things work better. For years, most of my adult life, I was vaguely surviving. To have snapped out of that would have been impossible. I have been coming to life slowly since my father's death, much as a person does coming out of anaesthesia. Words alone would not have brought me out. Tyler, and this home, have, which he permeates, ever-changingly.

This home, which trapped him at times in the past, and which he fought so hard to keep, feels right in every way to me, from the many collected treasures to my own place in it. I don't know everything on purpose, trusting as ever that things will reveal themselves as they need to. They do. I have sought a home within myself; now there is also one that surrounds me. It is the slowing down, the time spent regrouping, that has allowed for it.

Ralph Kramden just quit his job on The Honeymooners marathon. The bag of money didn't solve the problem in the end, but he was a millionaire for two days. The country now is in Kramden's shoes, having to take back the suits. We are communally at the moment before repossession, on this New Year's Day. What will save us is a sense of humour, and the buffering of the senses that has been in place for years.

I am grateful for the old TV set. In time we'll paint the house, most likely, one wall at a time, but when we do it will be with discounted paint. Times have changed. Abstinence is in. The converter box did the trick. In Romania, my niece Alexandra has already surpassed my technological level. That has to be alright. Ioana is editing film on her new computer. I have stood still. Running to catch up doesn't appeal to me anymore.

This quiet time almost over, the fire dying down in the early night, a magic show on TV, I drink my hot chocolate made with milk lovingly by Tyler. Tomorrow I will get a massage at noon, I will deposit checks in the bank and heal with my hands, in the evening. The storm of illness that settled over my body for days is over. Tonight I will sleep well. I have pulled through.

      The colours of the season, the red in CookieO'Puss' fur, shape themselves into the quilt that covers my legs and the decorations on the tree. Tyler's wearing his ruby robe, which I mended only days ago. Without opulence, there is comfort and grace. For years, my life was about accomplishing something, anything, so as to justify the expense of my life. Things have simplified, thankfully. It will take a little longer, but not much. I do not need to be more, to do more. At work, I will concentrate on healing. I have 'lost' over five hundred dollars by staying home this week, but sound planning made it so that my expenses for the home front are still covered for the next two months.

      I needed that certainty with the oncoming trip east. Between now and the time of departure I will only earn enough for last minute expenses, and when we return there may be new debt, but my footing has been established firmly.

      Tyler takes me as I am, and I him, without any more strain. I will not work as hard. That is part of love too, not just the things we do for each other. Details, meals cooked and shared, baths taken with familiar sounds in the next room, half a chord of wood used up, gloves taken out of a bag in the closet for inspection and use. We are at the bottom of the second box of Danish cookies, having had a fine Christmas time of year. Another round of news, and I am off to bed.

      On an office afternoon in the New Year, the last of the candy sits in the transparent jar on the desk, wrapped in red tinsel. It's always been hard to take the last one. When I stayed at Catherine's so many years ago I rearranged the candy in the dish, having picked and eaten the best one. It was important not to be found out, although it wouldn't have made any difference. On the other hand, when we used to go visiting in Romania in the seventies it was always important to eat all the sickly-sweet jellies people served. Tyler brings out cake and candy on a plate, so neatly, after dinner. There is the sense of simple abundance, with Tyler's daily bargain shopping. And still, I will not take the last piece of candy.

      Cindy offered me gum, the first I've had in months. I had some delicious soup-of-the-day from next door again and laid down to rest in the back. Towards the end of the day now, I am thinking of the repeated cooled reaction of someone who now knows about my being bipolar and has not scheduled more massages with me despite raving about my work in the past. I tell myself that 'I know that I don't know,' Recovery-style, that I could read anything or nothing into it.

      The difference from a year ago is that my heart didn't drop as it would have as a result. That is a lot. I have disclosed the same to two other clients, and when we return from our trip their reaction will settle only whether I should continue to be 'honest' in this way professionally. It is a risk, but it is important to know either way at this early stage. It will always depend on the individual, but if there is a consistent trend I will not be able to ignore it.

No matter what happens, I have such a clear sense of love in my life now that the rest of my life will turn into a continued apprenticeship more than anything else, and when it will be done there may finally be no more. It was such a joy knowing that much this past early morning, and waking up from my nap. I am a woman now, I know how to be secure and am secure consistently, and I have unconditional love on my side, freely given and received. All is well.

As usual, I didn't sleep on the flight. It was fun having Tyler order more and more Scotch until we got off in Dusseldorf and it was time to walk a straight line. On the second leg of the journey, on the smaller plane to Bucuresti, I still couldn't sleep but it was good to see Tyler resting next to me. I would nap later.

Spending time outside of the family on this trip will be the beginning of something new for me. I know myself better now; I take time to meditate again, I spend essential time reaching out to friends. There were so many warnings in the past with so little substance, that I was supposed to heed. It will have to stop here as I turn forty-two next week.

We have come a very long way to the medieval citadel of Sighisoara. Not only have we survived as a couple, but we're thriving. In this very quiet, wonderful place we are able to be ourselves outside of our comfort zone. Just now, having rested for hours in the afternoon, I have been listening to one of the staff at this inn complaining on the phone, through the wall, about a patron who came in with muddy boots and got the comforter dirty. Today, the cobblestone streets are wet with the aftermath of so much melted snow. It has been unusually warm. We rest and go out again. Melania, who works with me at Massage Envy, sent us to her relatives here. Gelu says there should be snow now, knee deep. He works in a cheese factory, and he is also a hunter.

A good salary in Romania is about three hundred dollars a month, which wouldn't even cover the heating bill in winter. Gas costs roughly four times more than in the States, and traffic crawls at best even on the intercity highways due to congestion. In the end many people are discouraged from traveling even what might seem to us short distances, and those who have to must deal with a certain sense of helplessness on a regular basis. It was good that Tyler and I decided to travel by train, and to leave Bucuresti for the more peaceful Transilvania.

Gelu says he could never live in Constanta, my birthplace by the Black Sea. It's too flat by the seashore for him. After making it to Transilvania, I can fully agree. Besides, the sea shore is out of control in the summertime with everyone flooding in. The summers have been brutally hot in Romania lately, so it has been so much more so. We will miss the medieval festival here in Sighisoara in July, but both Tyler and I are glad to have the place all to ourselves for now.

Claudia works in the Finances building downtown. Their son Alexandru studies at the German Lyceum at the very top of the citadel. He has to climb up the hundred and seventy hooded steps to get there every day. He also plays tennis and is very good at it, and knows PhotoShop inside out.

Gelu introduced us to the owner of a cellar where special Romanian brandies are for sale. Palinka is a refined version of tuica, a brandy which is commonplace, made generally out of plums. Tyler opted for some palinka from only last year, humble to his own beginner status. It takes time to know the difference. Then we had a leisurely lunch of pizza and beer, and mineral water for me. We wrote sixteen postcards between the two of us, on top of the ones we wrote in Brasov, which is a few hours away. We spent our first night in Transilvania there.

Now it's dusk. In the morning Gelu and Claudia will come and pick us up by car, at the inn. We will go to their home for a visit, then they will take us to the station for the trip back to Bucuresti to celebrate Ioana's birthday.

On the train, a woman was telling me stories. There's Crucea Caraiman, a cross mounted on a crest which has been there since the 1800's and which the Communists didn't dare tear down because it is a historical monument. Old steam locomotives like the one we just passed in a station were introduced in 1918 and were used into the early sixties. Then Diesel engines were introduced, and finally electric ones after 1970. In Azuga, a mountain resort, they built a ski slope in the year 2000.

Today we traveled in an old compartment. I was hoping we'd experience this kind of train car on this trip. I was reaching into my past with this faint hope, and luckily it was granted. Romanians are embarrassed by forty-year-old train cars that never got a fresh coat of paint, and admittedly the bathrooms in these old cars leave so much to be desired, but I was granted the wish to experience as an adult a little of what I used to know on the trains with my grandmother, on all those trips to and from the eye clinic. I knew better than to look for Nonna, but some of the old feeling of meditative longing to be with her translated into the present.

The fact that Tyler and I have come here together has made all the difference. I don't have to wonder what he may think about what I see, because he is right here and he tells me. I have a little of the prevailing defensive attitude of Romanians in this respect, it having been ingrained in me since childhood, but Tyler has made it clear that I don't need to. He loves me and he loves Transilvania. He loves the psychedelic effect of the aged tuica too, even more so than whiskey now, his favourite of so many years. And he is putting Sighisoara on the same par as Dublin, which says everything. It is a joy to see him take everything in, charming the natives as he goes, including animals and children. He is himself, at ease, and his pace matches his surroundings exactly.

Pulling into Bucuresti we were already fifty minutes late for Ioana's birthday party. Mioara was waiting on the platform. She had bought orange roses for Ioana on my behalf. It was lucky that she thought of it for us. Kiki was waiting in the parking lot. Before we could pull out onto the main street, someone who wasn't paying attention backed right into us, cracking his bumper and potentially pinning Tyler if there had been any speed involved. To avoid further delay, the two drivers decided on the spot not to file a report and we went on our way.

Tension filled the car, after we'd had such a nice time on the train. The word that describes Kiki's driving best is frantic, though dangerous and jolty fit too. To save time in traffic which is hard to imagine for Americans, Kiki decided to drive along the tram tracks as we reached Ioana's neighbourhood. That might have been alright except that at a certain point the cement lining the tracks gave way to gravel with little warning, and we were suddenly marooned on top of one of the tracks.

There was disbelief at first. Not only had that never happened to me or Tyler, but it hadn't happened to Kiki or Mioara either. We were trapped and there was the possibility of serious injury to the oil pan and the engine. Tyler watched on, stunned. I got enough of an adrenaline rush from it all to want to help, which in the end I did when about six 'lads' and I pushed the car backwards off the tracks. Mioara was calling Ioana and Razvan, her brother, to come tow us out.

People stopped or slowed down to shout insults at Kiki. Then, as quickly, the crowd dispersed, Mioara gave the man who helped out the most a tip, and we transferred roses and luggage to Razvan's car as fast as possible so as not to block traffic any more. Tyler and I piled in, Kiki and Mioara headed for home, and we were off with Razvan and Ioana.

After the introductions with my father's side of the family, we sat down to eat. Some of the food had turned cold, but the feast was on. It was difficult for them to believe how little we eat, and I was glad to explain again that we love food but we just don't eat much of it. Unlike others, they didn't push. The tuica came out, and with time Tyler felt better. Ioana was "smoking on down," as Tyler put it. She is the only one in the family who still does.

For once I didn't have to be the one representing the United States at the table. Ioana, Razvan and his wife Mihaela have all seen parts of the United States with their own eyes. Ioana worked for CNN in Atlanta years ago, and Razvan and Mihaela came for a visit in '96. But they wanted to know from Tyler how it's possible for an entire nation not to overthrow Bush's corrupt government for so many years, being that on paper at least the United States is still a democratic country.

Tyler patiently explained his own sense of civic duty and lack of respect for Bush. Being eager for a live link to the West, the other Dumitrescus didn't mince words and were able to overcome their inhibitions about speaking in broken English. I was proud of all of them and only corrected a word here and there.

Then we had cake with candles which Ioana blew out, and Razvan and his family were getting ready to go home for the night. Alexandra, his little girl, charmed us and was charmed in return. She is a gifted artist and a good dancer, aside from being so very beautiful.

Tyler, Ioana and I took the dogs down for a walk. Bila, Ioana's fourteen-year-old shepherd, is hanging in there. He liked his new tennis ball toy. It is understood that sometime soon Ioana will have to let him go but she isn't ready to, yet. When it was time to go back upstairs, Ioana picked up her massive shepherd in her arms and marched right up to their third floor apartment with him.

In the morning I took an early bath, wrote a couple of emails on my cell phone and took down some notes. Ioana had lent me and Tyler her bedroom while she slept in her study. Around seven o'clock her mother Antoaneta came into the living room where I was, and started up a conversation. In time Ioana woke up and came to join us. By nine they were ready to brew some Turkish coffee and Tyler was ready to have some too. I haven't had caffeine in a long time.

Eventually Tyler and Ioana and I and two of the cats and Bila were all in the study, by Ioana's computer as she checked world news, and later as I transferred images from my digital camera. I decided to take a chance and set up a website for the trip to Romania, and Ioana agreed to contribute to it by editing video footage, in time. It was exhilarating to have things flow so well, dispelling myths often associated with Eastern Europe.

In the afternoon, Razvan and Alexandra came over. Later they took us back to Kiki and Mioara's apartment. I needed a nap, Tyler stayed with me, and later Kiki broiled a whole chicken for us. There was no rush to get up early on Monday, so we stayed up till three in the morning talking. Since I'd put a load in to wash in the bathroom, Mioara and I were able to go off on our own after a while, put everything up to dry, and had a talk of our own while Kiki was holding forth and Tyler was holding his own. As we talked, as in the past, Mioara proved very insightful and supportive of me.

It is a dire time in Transilvania. In this place, Sighisoara, which is more beautiful than we could have imagined, a sense of frozen panic is seizing the population. Our friends here have jobs, but the sense of economic crisis is spreading both locally and nationally so fast that people are already visibly preparing for the worst. There is nowhere to turn.

      Earlier today we asked Gelu to drive us to Danes, just outside of Sighisoara, where he and Claudia took us last week. There are stables there, a restaurant and a little resort. The restaurant was nearly empty, though there was a table ready and waiting for a banquet in the smoking area downstairs where we ate, as we were surrounded by local antiques. In the end we didn't ride any horses, but it was lovely to see them, from ponies to a great charcoal stallion. They had been waiting patiently for their midday meal when we got there.

      Young women here wear high-heeled boots and jeans with lots of zippers, boasting drop-dead petite figures for the most part. Most women over a certain age wear babushka scarves and dull coats, dour expressions. People seem alert but unsure of how to proceed in general and in particular. There was a news report a few nights ago of people trampling over each other, Walmart-style, somewhere in a supermarket over a piece of free meat. In these parts, that is mostly unthinkable, but on the other hand anything out of the ordinary, including me and Tyler at the local market or on the train, can draw persistent stares. I have my Recovery training to help me, but it is still a challenge to act as naturally as I'd like to.

      In the citadel, people are prepared and very welcoming. At least now, as opposed to in Communist times, they are allowed to approach foreigners if they choose. It is also baffling for them that when we do ask for something, my Romanian is fluent and almost lacking in accent; but most of all it is strange for all involved that we should be here on vacation when Rome is burning, as it were. I can see how it could seem unfair that we should have the means to travel when more and more people here turn to begging.

      Still, there is a stoicism here in Transilvania among the people we met ourselves that is impressive, if not astounding. Although people are starting to prepare for the worst, which is yet undefined, they are doing so without the frantic approach of people in Bucuresti, for example. They tend to think before they take the next step. Alex, Gelu and Claudia's son who is sixteen and one of the most refined Europeans I've ever met, is going to be on exchange in Germany in June. Life continues because it has to, much as in the States, but with more poise.

      When we return to Newark on Monday, Mark will be in Florida and his wife will pick us up instead. He sent me a text message. We have missed the winter storm of the year. The irony of coming to Romania laden with warm clothes and finding balmy weather, only to hear about the storm in New York after we left, is uncanny. My artificial fur finally got a little wear after hanging in the closet for years, but for the second stretch in Sighisoara I borrowed the windbreaker I bought for Kiki at the Leader store. Tyler is sorry to have missed the snow, both here and at home.

Sighisoara is a wonderful place to rest. When we got in the other night and Claudia and Alex picked us up at the station, they brought us straight to her parents' apartment. They are staying at their home in the country for the winter.

We may get to visit them before we leave. Melania's word was enough for them. They opened their homes and their lives to us and hoped only to be treated as human beings. It is important to uphold this universal custom, and we are all doing that in this little circle.

Here on the desk beside me is Gelu and Claudia's studio wedding picture in black and white. The simplicity of the unframed print makes it extremely available, but I don't dare pick it up. People plan their lives here and hold to them. It is a joy to know them even in these hard times.

There is no phone and no TV in the apartment. There is peace and quiet. At the market tonight Tyler returned to being a smart shopper for the meal of snacks he prepared. The stove isn't turned on either or he probably would have cooked. Walking around we got the aroma of wood fires here and there from the houses peppered between apartment blocks. We will need to get more wood ourselves when we get home. Overall, we have been much warmer indoors in Romania than in our own home this winter. So much for this aspect of the myth of a backward country.

The young people are going to bear the brunt of the economic crisis here too, as they will in the States. They are not far behind, either. Most have techno knowledge, own cell phones and can access the Internet. They don't seem to have the public library system we have in New Jersey, though. Claudia was surprised when I described it to her. At the same time, old-style communication is very expensive. Letters and even postcards to the West cost more than a pint of beer does at the market. But there is a calling plan which allows people to call the US for free between 6pm and 8am on land lines. Many people have relatives in the US, since many Romanians have sold all their belongings for a chance to move to America only to find themselves falling on hard times even before the onset of the recent meltdown. Now they have nothing to return with and to. As ever, it is those who hold their ground who prevail and survive.

In these parts, which were dominated by the Austro-Hungarian empire for so long, there is what one might call a more civilized approach overall. In the citadel square, Tyler took me into a cellar store to buy me a birthday present. The antique belt that would have been his first choice cost over three hundred dollars, and we both opted not to get it. We spent a tenth of that instead on a hundred-year-old woolen handbag which will become one of my few prized possessions.

Things in the shop were piled high for every taste and budget, including sheepskin long coats, also very old, embroidered with traditional patterns. The woman told us that it is documented that those particular coats were worn only to church and on holidays, and that one of the two had been bought with the money from the sale of a cow. The more expensive one was being sold for five hundred dollars. Anywhere in the West it would belong in a museum, but here it hangs patiently outside the shop in the fresh air. People would have to come and get it here, literally, because international shipping costs are forbidding and eBay does not exist. Things are sold for cash only, for now, and those of us who do come in person can afford only to look. The Catch-22 is complete. Helmets from Austro-Hungarian guards at the turn of the last century sit, piled on top of each other.

On my forty-second birthday, just before noon, we are still in the apartment in Sighisoara, resting. It is sunny out, not too cold. We will not ride into the countryside with Gelu today. Something has come up. Tyler would have liked more of a plan to stick to, but we have both accepted the situation. I am a bit sleepy, grateful for the general decrease in pain in both my shoulders. We hear the national four-lane traffic outside the window in the living room. Tyler is dozing. We may meet up with Claudia and Alex later to celebrate my birthday in town, depending on what kind of day she's had. Yesterday was brutal, Gelu said. Over eleven hours of meetings, all related to the economic crisis.

On our walk up to the citadel we will find a place where we can buy an envelope for Bebe's letter, hopefully find our way to the train station to reserve our places for the ride to Bucuresti tomorrow, and get more Halls drops for my throat, which is still a little chalky. At six o'clock tonight we want to be at the clock tower, where the one figurine will come out holding two lit candles, signifying the end of the day. The torture museum is closed, and there are only the historic Ram's Head and Wagner pubs to try yet, but we would be allowed in to the lyceum building at the top of the hill, might even see Alex there. In time, we will come back.

As we approached Brasov, Bucuresti-bound on the train again, the landscape reminded me of southern Jersey. Then suddenly there was snow. I used the last of the battery in the camera to take some shots. Soon it was dark. Dr.Keyser called but I didn't get to the phone in time. When I checked my messages, Jamal had called too to wish me a happy birthday. A young girl in our compartment was talking the whole time to a school mate. His father checked in on them at one point.

There's still the mellow feeling of Transilvania on the train, and talk of an unknown America among the kids. Tyler has gone for a walk through the train. He's never seen snow in the mountains, except in Christmas cards. We'll have to go to the Rockies now too, now that I've seen that look on his face. I can't help wanting to stand by him, by creating new worlds for him if I can. They say children thrive in suitable environments. He does too. Such a private person normally, he has been fully able and willing to adapt to all the environments he's encountered here. He loves people who are not pretentious, or throw things in his face for no reason.

        I am weary of Kiki's behaviour and that's bad. I thought I was done with all that. Maybe we'll be able to salvage something, at least for Mioara's sake. It was important not to take a last-minute handout from my mother through them. The birthday party is tomorrow, and Monday we leave.

As we wait in the airport for the flight to Munich, we see more beautiful Romanian women in high heels and boots. Pittsburg won the Superbowl in the last minute of the game. We found out in the morning, since none of the cable channels broadcast it. Tyler cried watching the Springsteen halftime show on UTube at Kiki and Mioara's.

We have paid Western prices for our drinks as we wait. It will take some time to dispel the polluted effect of the last couple of days with Kiki. The experience with him was a direct throwback to what things used to be like when both my parents were alive. Mioara was lovely and positive in general, though she had to jokingly point out to me that I'm a Romanian who's not a Romanian anymore, because I didn't eat what she put in front of me the last night.

I'm sure she had no idea of the effect of that statement. I have been told so often that I don't belong elsewhere, that it hurts even more to be told in my native tongue that I don't belong in my native country, either. It was one of those deep pockets of pain they used to talk about at PRH in Edmonton. Kiki and Mioara wanted us to come, insisted that we stay with them instead of with my father's side of the family, and then tried to set us straight and curb our behaviour throughout. We were polite every step of the way, but there will not be a return performance.

Tyler loves flying. I don't. Cabin pressure is too much for me again in the small plane to Munich, but I will put up with anything to get home. 'It is difficult to be comfortable in an uncomfortable situation,' as they say in Recovery. I no longer feel that I have anything to prove, more so than ever, but this is something I will have to explain in detail before I put the whole matter to rest.

I am tall, athletic, beautiful and at ease. I give Claudia a lot of credit for being the only woman on this trip who accepted me fully. Others had different points of reference which made it hard for them to be impartial. More than ever, I am reminded that I need to consider people one at a time, not as a nation or a group. More than ever, I can tell myself that I did my part. If I had reacted at all to some of the provocations along the way, my temper would have been thrown back into my face, but being aloof and well is not acceptable either. Thus the polluted feeling.

Certainly I will have to think more of myself in general. I have been too generous and too open until now, probably because I've felt a need for approval. I no longer feel the need to apologize for being Romanian after this trip, to Westerners, or for having left Romania, to Romanians. I can say that because I found myself showing genuine interest in my surroundings as I went. If anything, I may have the role of an interpreter between the two worlds, one knowledgeable and impartial enough to make a difference. Something will come of the website, I have no doubt, even if it takes years.

In the meantime I will return to doing good massage work, improving my skills in general, and keeping a positive attitude in the midst of the current global crisis. I am entirely certain of it. The suspicious glances and cutting comments so common in Romania will fade, and the essence will rise to the top.

Eugen liked my writing. That is a lot. When things have settled, this installment of life will make its way into print. In Romania self-publishing is still rare, and even the initiative to do so seems strange and remote. With an economic future which is more uncertain than ever, people are behind in their debts as it is. Jobs are hard to find, and incomes are fixed if at all present.

I, on the other hand, can improvise to some extent back home, with massage work for one. It is a good thing to have given myself the freedom which stems from certainty in my own healing abilities. Unfortunately it is impossible for me to translate this gift to others. Some who already have it recognize it and understand, but those who insist on separation from it miss out for good. Something as simple as adjusting one's work to one's life instead of the other way around, with faith in the resulting beneficial effect, seems naive to Romanians and Americans alike.

But with faith, it works.

In Munich, the flight is packed and late but the captain says that conditions are favourable for making good time anyway. Almost there. There is plenty of energy at the start. "Here we go, sweetie!," says Tyler. Seeing a few shots of myself from our trip, it finally dawns on me that I have Eastern European features. With my long hair now, the picture is complete. Tyler has been telling me this for months, and that he's always wanted to end up with an Eastern European, but I must have been trying to distance myself from this imprint of my national identity until now. However, I am unusual in that I have childlike sparks in my eyes and lack that dour expression. No wonder I confused so many women on the trip, as often happens also in the States.

It's not unusual for people to want to do away with what they don't know. Tyler and I were both more concerned with having a good experience than fitting any particular expectation. Interestingly, there is a consensus even among the majority of Romanians that Westerners are more civilized than they are. That is the beginning of the problem. Technical improvements in themselves are assumed to bring progress at a personal level, but often civility is thrown out with old habits.

It used to be that Romanian girls had a dowry at any social level. One of everything was enough. They would bring something into their married life and go from there. Now if people have only one of everything it is more likely to be due to poverty alone. The Western longing for more has been fully accepted, bringing a growing sense of insecurity and malaise at a personal and national level.

For the sake of progress, animal farms have been all but eliminated; people in Romania are now eating chickens pumped with hormones just like Americans do. Despite the high price of gas, everybody who can drives, eager to save time and energy but finding they have less of both, just like Americans do. The major businesses in Sighisoara have been sold to Russians, Germans and other foreigners, since the amounts offered dwarfed local incomes to such an extent. Gelu is holding out for now when it comes to his land in Danes. Not many Romanians can.

As we get ready to reenter the United States, certain aspects of democratic life present themselves. When I asked a steward on the way to Europe if we needed custom forms for Germany, he said "Germany is a free country." On the way back, they gave us customs forms way in advance. Tyler is hot, I'm tired, but after we get home tonight I'll go get CookieO'Puss, we'll take a bath, and in the morning I'll go to work in Woodbridge.

The thought of our home is extremely comforting. Antoaneta was right: if Tyler hadn't come to get me, I would have continued to serve my mother and little else. In one year, Tyler has helped me build a secure life I couldn't have dreamt of, which no family members can dispel. I will no longer subject myself to what has been in the past. This trip was an effort worth making.

We got home on Monday night to urgent messages from Tyler's bank to call them about one of his accounts. When the smoke cleared it turned out that the government had put a freeze on that particular account, due possibly to an internal error at the bank. Days later we went in together, and called the police to witness Tyler's complaint, on advice from Tyler's lawyer.

The bank personnel and the police promptly tried to put both of us on the defensive instead, citing the Patriot Act which allows for such situations now as a very good thing, worth the trouble if it stops even one terrorist. The fact that Tyler has been banking at the same institution for thirty years doesn't count in such cases, since the different branches of the bank operate so remotely from one another. At the end of the day the funds were restored, but we may still put in a complaint with the ACLU.

It has been cold and snowy since our return, until today, when it should go up into the fifties. In Bucuresti it has been very warm for the past few days. It is Sunday. Soon we will take Ken's battery charger back before I go in to work at Massage Envy. It seems that we have turned a page for the better there.

With the money that I didn't spend on the trip I was able to erase my remaining debts here at home, which made me very happy. I have learned the value of money over the past year from Tyler, and now again in Romania. There, people must live on the salaries they have. They still look forward to government pensions, which have been provided for decades.

Gelu is my age, and so is Claudia, so by the time they reach the right age there may be no more pensions even there. The Romanian economy is collapsing because banks are not lending there either, businesses have no funds to pay taxes with, and are folding without the bankruptcy safeguards in place in the United States. If anything will allow the Romanian population to continue to function, it will be their ability to revert even at this late hour to the bartering they did during the '80s, when Ceausescu refused to import anything from the West so as to limit spending.

People would have starved if they hadn't traded and bartered. I say 'this late hour' for two reasons: one, by entering the European Union recently, Romania as a whole has accepted standards which seriously hamper old ways of trading, and two, with 'freedom' came Western ways of incurring debt at a rate which had not been possible before. Credit card debts and high mortgages are a reality in Romania too; the foreign companies that once paid high wages, allowing for high spending, are either drying up or leaving the country. Many families have cell phones and computers, paying Western prices for both, and the thirst for information about the West is greater than ever. But for now, a stupor of malaise is settling in. That is why it is more poignant than ever that Tyler and I were received so well overall.

A week after our return, something has been taken from me again as I sit behind the desk again in Woodbridge. My mother would still not let me have my life. She was invited to dinner at our house on Sunday, along with three of our friends. Neither Tyler nor I made any attempt to curb her tongue, hoping for the best. Towards the end of dinner, at the table, she went into a tirade about her sister-in-law Antoaneta, in a way that not only put Antoaneta down but also put me in my place for trying to be objective. Then she insisted that I put on the traditional top my aunt Cristina gave me, for show. Before everybody left she made sure I showed them the paintings of Tyler that I finished not long ago.

Tyler insists on patience with her because she is the person who gave me life. He is grateful to her for that. That is wearing thin now. She will cut deep to try to make sure I live life the way she wants me to. Despite setting a bad example in terms of bad health practices and lack of financial responsibility, with a general lack of compassion overall, she has the domineering insistence of an old world mother that is completely out of place.

I wanted to die again yesterday and this morning, even on the drive to work, as a result, like I used to every day for years while my father was still alive. I don't belong in Romania, being too free and open, I don't belong here, being too foreign, and if I were to believe my mother I would not belong in my own skin because I don't get paid enough doing massage work, and haven't 'made it' as the brilliant portrait painter that I am. There are no in-betweens for me, but my sister can do no wrong, no matter how much she goes into debt, stresses her body, etc. Family in Romania tell me that it is still on me that my mother counts more, but the way she does it is demeaning and draining to such a degree that I have no choice but to opt out. She would restore in me the insecurity of the past, by insisting on control over me.

I thought it was over, but it goes on. Again, I can only hope to be done with this world and never return, at times like these. When people tell me one particular person can't account for my depression to this extent, I ask them to think again. Although now there is only my mother, it is enough. Some life was restored to me with my father's death, and Tyler has revived me fully since, but my mother's death in life persists and she would bring me down with her.

Racial injustice does not go away when buried, publicly or privately. One's skin color doesn't wash off. In Romania, for children of inter-racial couples the mark of bias is there for life. I think that's what Antoaneta was trying to tell me that morning. Two nights ago Tyler played Olivier's Wuthering Heights for me, which drove the point home even more. One of my co-workers is dealing with daily racial bias, and the pressure has already risen to a critical degree.

Again, I return to one of my themes: being exposed to the world, I take people as they come individually. Gypsies ate all the legendary swans off a Viennese lake, threw a woman's body off a train in Italy not long ago, and they go around Europe saying they are Romanians whenever arrested. The bias against them in Romania is enormous. As a race they have drifted and survived since they left India hundreds of years ago. But at a personal level, the individuals I know who are of gypsy descent are self-respecting human beings who have built a place for themselves in society despite major obstacles. I respect that in part because of my own underdog status.

In inter-racial America there is a pattern of striking similarity in terms of social injustice towards people of colour. The generational shame placed on those who have not been able to rise economically is crippling, leading so often to violence and abuse. For those who do 'make it' there is pressure to separate from their origins much like the pressure my father would have imposed on me, to cut myself off from my Romanian past.

The problem, a good problem I think, is that it doesn't work. I can liken the situation to an infection which is never fully cleaned or treated, erupting periodically, or a bone fracture which was set badly, so that the limb remains crooked for life. In my case, the problem is mental illness. The bone had to be broken again repeatedly for some resolution to come, and now it has, but my mother would have me go back to what was.

When Tyler and I discussed making our home off-limits to my mother for awhile, so that I can be sure of a true safe haven for myself, he understood and granted my request. He is much more diplomatic and aware of the whole picture and I respect that. But my mother managed to make me vulnerable again to her whims in my own home the other night, and that has to stop, regardless of the financial circumstances. If I do not do this now, before I become comfortably self-sufficient and it would no longer be an issue, I would have been beaten beyond a point of death to such a degree that I would not be able to fully reclaim my existence.

It used to be that I needed validation, and that I found it most of all through writing. Now there are only traces of the pressure there used to be, to prove myself. I can bide my time, count my pennies, be a smart shopper. In time this last chapter of my old life will make its way into print and I will not waver. My mother has had an all-or-nothing scenario in place for me all along, taunting me to prove myself, but with this trip completed there is only the need for a true safe haven. Luckily it exists, and how. This morning, with my cat faithfully laid out on my lap and Tyler asleep in the next room, I can let the old world go without separation.

6.

I stepped off the side into the depth of the pool, anticipating the rush. Stepping back out, cold, I pulled at the edges of my suit. The sun brought instant relief, dulling looks that might have been directed at me, going to work immediately on warming my flesh. The thought of Tyler, even before I reached his eyes, filled me with confidence. Now I go to expressions stored in my mind of his pride in me, of love, and my footing in the world is reaffirmed.

There was a group of boys at the concession stand who would have needed fifty cents. They were considering their options when I stepped up to get soda for my mother. Someone might go home for it, they thought out loud. I wanted to hand them the change since I had it, but stopped. It would have been inappropriate for me to resolve the issue for them. Once I gave a public worker a bottle of juice that was my only treat for the day, in the days when money was tighter. Now, with money to spare, I held back. Elders I learn from sometimes watch without interfering, but something still rips in me when I don't share all I own.

My mother took the time to criticize my gait, noticing my left foot bending out in my old shoe. She said I should try to walk straight anyway though the one leg is shorter, the day was lazy and the shoes were very worn. Then she said "Look, the fifth one fatter than I am, today! Shame on her!," returning to her main obsession.

As I see Tyler's joy in the things he loves I get courage to hope for what I might need too. I have learned simple appreciation again, for everything from the car that didn't die, to the new wallpaper we put up, to clearing my own bills. As we've run from doctor to doctor with my mother for weeks, it is Tyler who continues to restore me to my life after the difficult exchanges I still open myself up to. The abuses of kindness can't go on forever, but while they do he is there. Most of all, Tyler gives me time when I need it, and lets me come to him.

A tone of voice changes, something is said in haste out of habit without ill intent, and I find myself needing to regroup in front of the computer screen, continuing an earlier project. I separate the trigger from the mechanism it set off and realize that I am reacting not to the current situation, but to a compilation of past stifled events. My emotional equilibrium is sensitive enough to the subtle waves of everyday language that I am brought back to insecurities that have already left me. A great sadness enters again, making me want to leave this world instead of participating in it, despite my usual interest and compassion. It is temporary.

At times like these I could believe my mother saying that I am ill, once again, because in being even a little floored I have been struck to the core again. The link always leads all the way back. The murkiness of it would make depression linger, but the mechanism for recovery is in place by now to such a degree that some time editing pictures is enough. I will not indulge in temper, and once again I will seek out the pain so that I can let it go. Once even a little on the way, I remember my commitment to myself. It is time to take it a little easier, backtracking once again to see my own tendency to take on too much, put expectations on others which will need to be disappointed, and the positive need for rest.

My mother may go join my sister for several weeks in Romania, and if she does that will be time to regroup. The other day she threatened to live another fifteen years as if I would object in any way. Lacking Quality in most respects, her way is by definition different than mine, but the tone which is there in her voice so often would demean both me and Tyler out of the meanness she was born to. I watch for that tone in her and do my best to guard against it, but it burrows in, taking days to dissipate fully.

I have backed away from some whom I considered safe until recently, too, realizing that perhaps I was wrong and trusted too much in them. Having shaken off another skin, I am more vulnerable at a time when much weight is put upon me again, and my hair turns a little whiter in my own image of myself. On the outside I smile, having learned to do that from Tyler.

It will be twenty-five years since Nonna died the way she said she would. I passed a bumper sticker that said "This car climbed Mt.Washington" and was reminded of my fifteenth summer. Our car had climbed Mt.Washington too, with the five of us in it. We were still trying then. Nonna was still alive, one of the sages who knew that her new setting of the house on Locust Drive was only temporary, that she would soon close her eyes at night chewing on her chocolate and not return the next morning. It would be two more years before she passed away, but she knew she would get her wish, that easy passing. She had carried our world long enough, when it was time, she had already let go. Yet even now, whenever I need her, she opens the door to memory again, and is with me, most of all her smile.

Tyler's warmth next to me as I make my early morning notes is suggestive to me of what might have been the warmth shared by the three baby cardinals in their nest outside our front door. Two days ago one got stuck in the garage against the back window and Tyler let me put on rubber gloves, put what might have seemed an enormous hand over its hind quarters and carry it back to the nest in the fuchsia plant. We had noticed the four eggs in the perfect nest inside the hanging basket weeks ago, when we needed to water it.

Then a campaign of cooperation started between us and the parents. They hatched late last week and have flown away now, but the experience brought out waves of unprecedented compassion from Tyler, whom I assisted in making the whole family comfortable. The kids became our kids, we were overjoyed that they hatched successfully and mourned when one made its way out of the nest too early and died after falling onto the step.

Mr. and Mrs. Cardinal watched from the corner ledge as I picked up their dead, unable to do more, and as Tyler and I buried him in the back yard next to where Tyler's mother's ashes are buried, as was her wish.

After that our hopes were with the other three, and on the afternoon when all three had flown out of the nest successfully for the first time, they were already going through vigorous take-off and landing exercises in the yard.

The parents' dedication to the young birds was unshakeable. Despite their wild nature, they trusted us, but not enough not to chirp beyond their size. They might have been giants in spirit. One young cardinal came out of a bush, too young to be afraid, feet away from us. We left him alone. An hour later the other one had to be rescued from the garage.

By the next day when I got home in the evening they had left the nest for the trees for good. Tyler had become the father of our children in my presence. He has been a father before, adoptively, in several relationships, but between us these may be the only children we will ever have. His own childhood wonder, care and concern affected me too. The honour of being chosen for the site of the nest, the birds' instinctual wisdom, has added strength and even more love to our own bond.

At the lawyer's today, my mother threw in my face again at the end of the meeting: "You still don't trust me, do you?" I had asked if after the new will would be finalized my sister would be bound by law to give me half of my mother's assets. When we got there, she put the case as her having given my sister everything up to now with the understanding that I would be given sums "as needed", and that I didn't like that. There was a closed meeting with just my mother and the lawyer, after which I asked the result and was told that the new will would have my sister as the executor still, and probably someone in the United States to represent her since my sister doesn't live here.

No, I don't trust my mother. On the way that morning I had found out that her will is weak enough to have her give herself the reasoning of stress over her possible thyroid cancer for the need to start smoking again. She had lasted a few days on the patch. Her lack of commitment to her own health speaks for itself. Then she was irritable as is often her way, ready to pour her stress over me and Tyler again.

What I wanted at the meeting was a lot more than the fifty percent of her assets, and a lot less at the same time: I wanted her respect. I, and lately also Tyler, have acted in good faith as decent human beings trying to help her through her current health crisis, as well as standing by her in general, despite the condescension and occasional insults. Not once was it mentioned during this time by her, though by many others, that I have become more responsible than her in many ways, in many respects, from pointing out banking issues that stood out, to helping with any and all technical difficulties, to taking her places.

My psychiatrist asked me the other day if this is an Eastern European thing, a mother picking the offspring she likes least to drain, and not recognize when recognition is due. That in itself is bad enough, but the real issue is insisting that I am not my sister's equal because I am bipolar.

My sister's spending behaviour, and averages of four hours of sleep a night, as well as waves of depression, characterize her as bipolar also, though she refuses to be diagnosed. Aside from that, I am taking care of our mother, with Tyler's help, and took care of both our parents for a full seven years leading to my father's death, with only weekly phone advice from her from overseas, while I was making my way towards a steady recovery and a full life of my own.

My sister moved to Switzerland permanently in 1989, the year I was diagnosed with bipolar disorder in New York. After that she saw my parents on holidays, contributing time in earnest only once, when my mother had her second hip replaced in the spring of 2007. At that time, when my father was already advanced enough in his Alzheimer's to frighten my sister's daughter Nicole nightly as he roamed around the house, my sister insisted on spending days obsessively cleaning the kitchen and the bathroom, planning substantial structural changes in my parents' house so it would sell, and being condescending towards me as ever. I will always be grateful for one thing: she allowed me to spend time with Nicole.

But months earlier, after two weeks of silence towards me at her home in Switzerland on holiday along with my parents, she spoke up in the last three minutes of the ride to the train station to tell me that I should move to Romania because I was costing the family too much. Clearly to her I was dismissible in the extreme, though she could not fire me as an employee outright, just try to intimidate me.

In the summer of my sixteenth year, she had established an even more profound basis for my lack of trust in her. Being a year older than me, she decided that she was more fitting for the high school senior I was in love with and had made friends with, a lifeguard at our local pool. She and another friend of ours had vowed to stay friends with Richard when he told us that he was going to have a very difficult year and would not really have time for a relationship, but privately my sister pursued him, making herself available physically, and within two months she told me that I had just been too young. A couple of years later, even before they broke up, Richard told me that if I had insisted myself at all it would have been me.

Earlier yet, still in Romania, when my sister was just nine or ten, she had started to feel the desire for walks with boys, and I was sent to tail them, never more than a few feet behind, by my mother. A pattern that I was never comfortable with was established, and once I tried to hit her date in the stomach. That day, my sister taught me something very important. She said "If you want to get me, do it with words, not with your fists." She was the bookworm at the time, I was the tomboy, so that was a form of complete dismissal which was only interrupted by the several months we spent at my grandmother's apartment in Bucuresti, waiting to join our parents in the States. She had almost not wanted to leave Constanta, our home till then, because of a boy.

My mother demands trust too, despite her own depression, which she acknowledges but refuses to seek help for, despite her tendency to bend to all her own weaknesses, not to speak of her behaviour towards my father while he was unable to defend himself in the last years. People have told me again and again that she is just hard, even harsh, that now that she's old and ill she needs me and I need to look over certain things. But when it is thrown in my face that despite acting more responsibly that most adults it is assumed that others have the right not to trust me in return, I will step back, as I am stepping back today. Enough is enough.

If I wait long enough the worst always passes. The teachings of Dr.Low, founder of Recovery in the 1930's, become even more integrated in my life as I follow his advice, using physical activity as a distraction from preoccupations. With time, the importance of asserting my will positively settles in, and then it is possible to conceive of training my will further. The will being such an important aspect of yoga work, it is very important for this to happen, but also for it to happen without strain or discord.

Much like fasting, as I understood it from my yoga teacher, this work should not be forced in any way, nor should information be crammed. It is that important for secrets to unfold, or perhaps only for truths we have been busy obscuring to make themselves evident. As much as I have felt this way before, I haven't had the words to shape the thought until now. Without a doubt, I must continue to slow down.

Meanwhile I have noticed a pattern that is too strong to ignore: for the most part, people need to find someone else to put down before they can feel secure in themselves, which naturally makes for a false sense of security. What is natural selection based on agility, age and intelligence in the wild is replaced among humans by systems for domination. But in our case, intellectual agility is not encouraged, as one might expect, or certainly not beyond a certain point.

Our educational systems, despite their claims, do not generally encourage emancipation and advancement; they generally fail to encourage a continued habit of self-education. Degrees are for the sake of careers, not self-development. Teachers are encouraged to conform, and are often marginalized if they don't. I've seen this in high school, then in college: children are encouraged to follow the path of the parents, which has often been softened and smoothed, instead of searching for their own.

In New York in the spring of 1992, just before I moved to Montana, I asked a gallery owner of some prominence to look at my slides of abstract landscapes and he did, after which he said "Pretty good, I could get you a show in about two years, but whom do you know in New York?" I had gone to the Cooper Union 'cold' out of high school, having made a sudden turn away from the honours track.

Many of my classmates had working artists in the family. I had successfully crashed the party and was allowed and encouraged to develop, but my training would have required further years of development beyond graduation, at which point my father had expected me to become a self-supporting artist. Marketing is everything in art as elsewhere, whereas I had just begun a long path to self-searching instead of financial independence.

Patrons of artists have always needed to be able to sell what become their wares at one level or another, and as times are getting harder they may have even less choice but to conform. I stopped painting with hope of being recognized or making a living from it long ago. The self-portrait finished the other day brought me all the more joy for that reason. The three portraits I did of Tyler last year and my own little one from last spring laid the ground work for this one. Luckily by now ability has become a given, but now there is life in my eyes on this canvas like there never was before, mirroring what goes on inside. I would sell it nonetheless, but only in exchange for things or services that would improve our home.

Our home is slowly waking up to its potential lately, the more we pay attention to it in our joint life. This weekend was momentous in that we emptied the unoccupied front room of most of the furniture. The bed had held the room in place these past twenty-five years since Tyler's mother's passing, gathering things and other furniture around it, deadening the space. With Bruce's exit we made the decision to transform the room.

Tyler worked diligently for weeks to separate, dust and move objects stored in the closet, so potent with memory that they had to be handled individually, each one allowing for floods of memories. Letters from before and since the Civil War had to be read, people identified in sepia-tone prints, objects handled with care. Then the new gear went in, massage-related, before the rest could begin.

To help things budge, I hardened my will and gaged the weight of things rather than their value, staying clear of the more glamorous aspects of things. Tyler has come to trust my organizational skills and manual dexterity, and gave me free reign, helping me as I asked, but only when I asked. He was reassured that I did not disturb the content of drawers when we moved cabinets, or the order of tapes on shelves. He bore any discomfort he might have felt with grace.

These many things for him to consider inside the house are his legacy, that for which he withstood the physical and mental abuse from his father and the emotional abuse from his mother. Daily, these many objects are both the clues to his eventual release and the daily re-enforcers of so many injustices. His pain is so deep that it carries from day to day, to be released daily by swimming and nightly by his rituals of filtering information deep into the night, saving events in time and in memory.

Stirring the dust in this way has begun a new process for both us: for me as 'the woman of the house', having lived previously in settings that were relatively barren, and for Tyler as witnessing his own potential for change. In the past, in my parents' home, I stumbled at best in my efforts to improve the layout of the furniture in the rooms or to set order in the pots and pans which found their way to chaos again by the next day. I would return to the order of my own apartment for the night and be drawn back by old ties of guilt and responsibility in the morning.

        Now, although by reflex I still ask Tyler for permission all along the way, I trust my decisions more. Physical work is necessary for me in the house so that I can walk from room to room and remember that I've contributed to it in some way. I remember the effort and am validated much like some men take pride in their cars. Having left a mark, I belong a little more in my surroundings, without the negative criticism or the fear of reprisals of the past.

A young girl peered through the window of the indoor pool, eating her ice cream from a cup methodically. She gave me a serious little nod of acknowledgement when she saw that I had noticed her, and went on eating. For the whole swim I thought of Nadia, who had looked so much like this girl when I met her in 1993. She had had the long blond hair and the studious nature too. Nadia smiled more though. The last time I saw her, in 1998, she still jumped in my arms to be held.

That was before the unthinkable damage was done, that Nadia kept to herself until she couldn't, anymore. It came out with the shorn hair, the cuts on her skin and cigarette burns on her arms. She had become numb to herself and needed the pain to remind her she was alive. Years have gone by again since my last contact with her, when things were already better. I feel a loss, not having been able to keep in touch with Nadia and my other Canadian friends.

This morning I inadvertently ran over and killed a squirrel that must have been sleeping just behind the front far tire. It is the first and only squirrel I've ever killed; I kill plenty of spiders now, creatures, as Tyler calls them, though in the past I would never kill them because my father objected. But then my father didn't have Tyler's history with spiders. Still, there is a sense of loss in any of it.

The young girl came back towards the end of my swim and sat on the bench again, draped in a leopard-print towel after her own swim. Then she was gone again. Living without kids, I can only imagine the responsibility placed on parents. Would this girl become a swimmer, like Tyler did? Would she have to convince her parents to let her, or would it be easy? Would she want to compete or was she instinctively drawn to the meditative aspects of lap swimming? On the first hot day of summer, she chose to look inside rather than out.

I buried the squirrel in the back yard. There are so many interwoven roots; the canopy of trees in our yard draws a great contrast to the moon-like landscape of fifty years ago, when Tyler's family moved in. He had had to mention the small corpse to me, I hadn't even seen it driving in. I may be becoming callous in my lack of attention, like so many other drivers in New Jersey. Later I will busy myself with soaking good oil into the floor of the front room, and that will bring me back to myself.

The reality of kids filing past as they get ready to do a dive is like an interactive game and no more. I am not quite part of it all. I don't need to cause myself physical pain to exist, but I feel removed. Something more is to come. Seeing the production of The Little Foxes on Tuesday night was more real than this. The actors fleshed out the words, the words painted a tale lost in time, and the tale was partly my life. The ending was the last of the life at Locust Drive.

Being so much of this world in its portrayal of chicanery and greed, the plot and the performance stayed true to the level at which most of us exist, with manipulation being at the forefront. Even in the sanctuary of this pool compound on a sunny day, I see with some apprehension what some people would like to preserve now: the precarious sense of balance that is slipping, that was so much more present here at this time last year.

My cousin Ioana told me over the phone that Romanians are not as worried as we are, probably because of the fifty years of living fully deprived, never knowing where the next injustice would come from. We Americans worry as a nation, though, no matter how much emphasis is put on the banal in the lives of the rich and famous.

It would be difficult for me to say whether outside the United States people are really less obsessed with fame and fortune or if that is just what I would like to think. My father wanted his fame and fortune over thirty years ago in Romania, so he brought us here to the U.S. That's why he brought us here. He didn't get it though.

His father had made himself a fortune, then had it taken away from him when all the laws that had existed were dissolved. And instead of gleaning from the experience that what is of essence is inner fortitude, my father looked outward for proofs of recognition for the rest of his life. His intelligence, his every effort guided him outward, so that insecurity led to domination of others, and rigidity.

As much as he imposed himself in various ways, he held no inner ground, and thus was always hungry for more. I say this not with disrespect, even with compassion. I couldn't have reached him, though I thought I should. He had gambled on getting recognition through accomplishment, and instead he succeeded in creating a labyrinth of behavioural traps which became worse over time. Did that lead to Alzheimer's? Maybe. His father had had dementia too. Certainly it made him an easy victim of neglect in the end.

For now it may be time to forgive my mother while she is still alive. I do not expect fairness, and never know what will come next, except that she will not at any time come to live with us. An hour in her presence produces the negativity that comes together in a week elsewhere. It is unclear how much longer I will accept financial help from her, due to limits on my work set by the slump in the economy which affects us all, but a slow steady sense of security has taken hold in my life already. Only rejection from Tyler could even begin to shake that now.

My mother has lost the grip she once had, of convincing me that I am less valid as a person because I live with a mental illness I was predisposed to genetically. It has been a long struggle, and I am still careful about disclosing "my record" or my writing on the subject. Many people aren't ready to hear the truth that I can function as well or better than them. I function like someone returning from a war into a world at peace. My war happened to be internal and is refreshed by my family periodically, but there are still horrors which are hard to explain to anyone who hasn't gone through them.

Taking a sensitive nature and trying to make it fit into a pattern it's not meant for is as much a crime as maiming someone with a physical weapon. At a spiritual level most of us know that taking a life will diminish our own, and that some healing must take place when the deed is done, that amends must be made. Often though, the shame of the mistake will carry into denial of wrongdoing, even to the point of repetition. If that works in war, it bleeds into addictions and other disorders on the outside. I struggle to overcome rigidity, others struggle to enforce it. Following all the rules, I am allowed to function. The regular channels do not allow for my reality, but there it is.

The notebook thins as notes end up in the computer, contributing to my current need to document, and then are discarded. No longer living on my own, I am faced with the need to hesitate or even to compromise my own creative life for the sake of things we do together, but in the process something even more interesting happens: I learn more how to live, how to interact, to break for dinner, or a walk or a day at the pool.

Left to my own devices I might go from canvas to keyboard to scrubbing floors with no interaction at all. As John Lennon wrote in a passage Tyler showed me yesterday, I'd be accomplishing things for others, still, instead of living for my own sake. This need I've inherited from my father, to accomplish more and more and more so as to become valid, is ever-present, but to be curbed. At the same time, now that I am well, balanced and loved, creativity gushes out on its own. Old patterns of stunted motion are giving way to the possibility of inter-connectedness of my interests: healing, music, art, writing.

With nothing to prove and no money to speak of to invest in further education or tools, I am left to observe my world at leisure. I notice things like our cat's withdrawal this morning in protest of a full day of neglect with the party yesterday, I notice the smallest bee I've ever seen flying by my hand. I notice the sun finally burning through lotion and wind to my muscles on another day of leisure at the pool. I notice how secure I felt within myself yesterday despite the inappropriate behaviour of a friend, without warning. Much like my sister long ago, she lost my trust for good in the process, but any insecurity related to the event is already passing. There can be security even in hesitation, after all.

Persig taught me about maintenance, Peter Brook taught me that hesitation is essential in acting, Dr.Low taught me there is only security or insecurity at any one time. Dr.Keyser gave me the concept of forgiveness as a necessity, and Tyler allows me into his psychedelic forays. My own groundedness takes me further as Alan Watts drops gems on our way to the shore. I am more ready to withstand the world all the time this way. Doing all this is as important to me as developing my talents in a literal sense.

Having lived and moved around as much as I have, I am detached from small-town intrigues. The fears I used to have living in my apartment have all but dissolved. I am disappointed that the local zoning laws will not allow me to do healing work at home, but even that will not bring me down. As I do more work, both physical and mental, I lay the groundwork for more to come.

In the past I would get frustrated because I didn't have the time and energy to do creative work, knowing full-well that the main reason for it was continuous emotional upheaval. Now I am able to take the part-act Recovery approach, planning projects in parts, allowing for relief in the way of a grocery run or a walk or a good night's sleep. Yes, there is always more, but the satisfaction of doing a task well at the time brings the kind of contentment I've always hoped for.

Through my straw hat and the sunglasses epoxied together for me by Mr.Greulich, I see people drifting around us in the field by the pool. There are pictures of me in this field as far back as twenty-eight years ago. Now I can just sit there, the same as I can just be at home as the neighbours make efforts to gather details about me. I can live with myself and walk with my head high.

Am I cured? Was I never ill? Dr.Keyser listens to me carefully at the end of every month, and he ordered routine blood tests for this week as he does every few months. With my mother on vacation far enough away, I can conceive of a time without daily strategic emotional blows. I know that the goal is to function despite them, but there is that key factor in Recovery thinking, of dynamic outer environment, that meaning those closest to us, of systems that reinforce weaknesses and insecurities in people with mental illnesses or psychological issues that are deep-seated. My old therapist used to talk about the mobile effect and the 'identified patient,' in which one family or group member would be set apart and allowed to struggle in vain once the brand was set.

A long-legged mosquito was struggling in the invisible web of a spider above our bed, one night, much in the same way. Tyler was sharing one of his late-night stories and I didn't want to interrupt. I would have had to go get a shoe and kill them both if I had, but instead I watched the much bigger creature struggle every time the spider drew near, backed off, and came back again. When we turned out the light they were still at it, but in the morning there was no trace of either. Normalcy had returned.

I could relate to the struggle though. In my hopelessness of the past I would often not be able to see far ahead. Now, ironically, my coming from a long line of engineers, as Tyler does, works in my favour. Using another Recovery concept, that of distracting my emotional self through physical action, having learned about humility where physical as opposed to cerebral work is concerned, I am free to enjoy every aspect of my life.

With this approach, taking up forty-year-old carpet is not a chore but an opportunity to uncover the beautiful wood underneath. Painting the walls and even the ceiling in "the new room" was a way of defining spaces, even creating a three-dimensional starting point for the work of reclaiming the house. We may be able to make that effort together.

It is a house of treasures on so many levels, and as the house comes to life, I see Tyler changing with it. As Professor Petlin taught me at Cooper, you start with broad strokes of good paint to set up the structure, moving around the canvas in unison of loose movement. Then details come in. For now, the loose strokes are my brute initiatives guided by Tyler's knowledge of the house, but he does the more important work of sorting through what was displaced.

About the time of my first episode in New York twenty years ago, I spent time in the old office of the Review, having called on Catherine for help. Before she was able to leave with me for the day, I tried to rearrange a nearby desk into perfect alignment, becoming paralyzed by my own actions as I did so. At some level the need to keep my muscles busy was there, which is not uncommon in manic states, but that wasn't my desk. I hadn't asked before going to work, and when it dawned on me that I might be punished for having interfered, and couldn't return it to its general disarray, I froze.

At the time my need for harmony and grace was abstract and palpable at the same time, with neatness being paramount. Now I leave people to their own messes, and the physical work as it comes dispels old taboos of manic behaviour, as it is measured and within reason. In our home everything has a purpose, whether that is to suggest a favourite memory by its physical presence or to be a handy tool for the day's work. Tyler puts things in historical context for me and we move on. In the end, it becomes clear that even neurological pathways can be readdressed. It is such a fundamental aspect of getting to know oneself but most of us can't shake off the dust or clutter we need to dispel to get at it, and yet it is available to any of us willing to do the work.

Just like the head of the hammer flying off the handle and killing Alan Watts' Satori animal, a moment of connectedness happened for me too the moment we set foot in Asbury Park today. Tyler is not only my mate, he is also my main vehicle for understanding. He puts things in my lap which fit, like the Alan Watts tape in the car today.

I have wondered about meditation in one way or another my whole life, tried to understand it, do it, do it right. There are rules, there is the need to pursue understanding, and then it comes back to what my teachers said at Cooper: learn all the rules so that you can let them go. My yoga teacher will not reveal too much, as he shouldn't, and he insists on personal contact, which has also worked best for me too.

Alan Watts reveals worlds of experience, on the other hand, knowing that only so little will stick, but in the right places. He found the joy which allows for constant playfulness and humour. I let his words in without separation this morning, feeling rested in the passenger seat. It did me good. Lately the teachers I've needed all along have come, as does the recurrent thought of my grandmother reminding me that between the two of us there was no separation.

I never thought I was or would be better than Nonna, but neither that I was any less. Whatever might be interpreted as my spiritual arrogance of connectedness to God originated thankfully from her allowing me to be part of her. I have sought that initial innocence of my childhood ever since my arrival in the new world, with little success. Until now. Now Tyler and I are children together, functioning in the world. If it is all that happens for the rest of our lives, it will be alright.

Gliding with him on the surf board, I laughed harder and more sincerely than I can remember laughing in a long time. One time we laughed about that trite beginning in so much writing, "It all began..." Well, it all begins here, in medias res, in the middle of things, where we are right now. Tyler already finished his ice-o-matic drink and is now listening to Linda on his headphones facing the ocean, already brown with the sun, packing more sand in a bottle to take home. I am happy to see him happy.

In so many ways, there is no more. We will struggle financially along with others, and when the time comes we will buy another chord of wood in the late fall for winter; Halloween will come. I will take care of Tyler the way Nora took care of Aiden, the best I can. I won't see too far ahead for awhile.

The fabric of our lives has not dissolved, on the contrary, we are strengthening it one strand at a time, with the sure knowledge that each one will affect the rest. Tyler writes at night surrounded by his things, I write whenever I can and bring it down later. He is the scholar, I live for the experience most of all. Here at Asbury Park today, I fit, as does Tyler.

The common denominator of tolerance is more easily found here, even than in Romania, where people are starting to take vacations on the Bulgarian shore instead of in my busy birthplace, Constanta, on the Black Sea. Rivalries continue to amuse me wherever I go, as between our town and a neighbouring one, having found parallels wherever I've lived. Each time the little universes seems all-important, but are not. Stereotypes and biases about Eastern Europe and especially Romania no longer feel like they apply to me, even when comments are made with that intent.

I will meditate in the car as I did in my childhood, make love in life and in my dreams, enjoy the occasional fried chicken leg despite having become a vegetarian recently, if my sweetheart cooked it on the 4th of July. Throughout my life I've shackled myself with the need to understand my surroundings, trying not to conform at the same time. I have subjected myself to rules that did not apply to me, taken on burdens that were not mine, though it had been pounded into me that they were.

I have tried to understand why my mother doesn't love me; by now I am finally ready to walk away from that question. The answer of "Of course I love you - every mother loves her child!" doesn't have the effect it once did. Now it is enough to wear my hat walking down the boardwalk on the way to get pizza in this waking dream of a summer day. Why did I ever think I needed more?

7.

The cavernous laundromat is no longer there, at the end of Brant Avenue. A bulldozer and a pile of dirt mark the spot in the parking lot. Pulling left onto Westfield Avenue again, I as if entered the laundromat again, as I had years ago. I had struggled with the feel of the place and never returned.

Rows of ill-kept machines had sunk into the back wall. A cold concrete floor had held on to water. Fluorescent lights had flickered. Somber people, familiar with each other it seemed to me, were functioning better than I was. I was surprised this morning to see that the memory of the place had stayed with me as much.

Things do, though the physical lack of the place gave rise to a small hope in me that other things would fade too. The house on Locust Drive has a new porch and shrubbery, and I no longer feel compelled off the Parkway exit up onto the hill heading that way anymore. The mailbox still would mark the spot for first-time visitors, but I will never have to give those directions again. What I might have let go of twenty-five years ago, I have let go of now.

A day before Thanksgiving, I hit a wall of pain in my new home. A bit tired, not having taken the time to let worries settle, I had said careless things. Walking in after the session with Dr.Keyser, I pulled money out of my pocket in an offensive way. Immediately afterwards, the surge of insecurity that came as a result brought an outburst of tears that I could not control, but I knew enough to ask Tyler to bear with me as I rested for the afternoon. Our cat climbed into bed right after me, providing the balance that I wasn't able to find on my own. Then life started over.

My own excessive expectations were exposed. Picking myself up, I saw my financial limitations no longer as fair or unfair, but as what was, at the moment. My mother may be mean, but that doesn't make her irrational. If she wants to cut me off altogether for having her driver's license taken away, that vindictiveness doesn't make her irrational. Going blind and holding on too tightly to the idea of independence through driving, my mother has been indulging in unprecedented "crazy-making" behaviour, as we used to call it in PRH years ago. But if she wants to write me back out of the will as she might fire an employee, I cannot stop her.

What I can do is just let her go. She is away in Romania again, making it easier for me. Hearing me say that I no longer fear her, sent my mother into disbelief. I am becoming my own person, finally, in my early forties. Meanwhile my mother is not struggling yet financially, despite a serious gambling habit which she admittedly cannot control. She knows I'm struggling though, and have all my life. She would break my will by withholding money, now most of all.

A few days ago, I may have mimicked my mother's behaviour through my own gestures towards Tyler. But with time and space, with rest, with Tyler's love and our cat's affection, we moved on to a loving Thanksgiving day. I had the feeling that I might be "honest" after all, with myself about choosing the work that I have, of healing, knowing that I didn't do so for the money; honest with myself about thinking I was entitled to certain things because I have talent as an artist, and because my parents could afford it. That had become about proving my worthiness, years ago. Now all that's left is this mean, though not irrational behaviour on behalf of my mother which makes me crawl into bed for hours before I can function again.

I comforted myself this morning, turning the corner again past the old laundromat, about how I've come along. Three years ago I had no more than forty dollars available three days into the month, not three days before the end of the month. My father was still alive then. I would gather just enough energy each night after a day spent with them, to head back to my parents' house in the morning. My apartment was my refuge, but it wasn't enough. The year before that, I had dared to pray that my father would survive a coma brought on by fever, and was held responsible for it by my mother and my sister. So I returned, every day, to be drained again, having to grovel for groceries, living in indentured servitude, yet being told by my mother that I wasn't needed.

Now I live for myself. Sometimes when I look up, there are still some who would have me return to arrogance and high expectations, perhaps because that is what they know well, or mistake for accomplishment. Not Tyler. "Pretend" is one of his least favourite words. He carries information daily, with a life-long approach, and he has a remarkable memory for facts and details. He will always make an effort to use language that is simple and direct, nonetheless. That helps me in my own choices of words. I am a little tired of finding occasional traces of superiority in the behaviour of random people who choose to see my faint accent in English first, and then what else I might have to share. When I was a teenager, my insecurities were heightened by these marks of self-appointed superiority. Now they tire me, no more.

The first sense of insecurity came with having horrors about world history instantly revealed at the age of twelve, as preparation for coming to the States. I had not known any of my family history until then. I had accepted the shelter I thought was reality, of a comfortable middle-class life in Communist Romania.

But my sister and I became second-class citizens even before we left Romania for the States, since my parents' defection had had consequences. The family left behind on both sides bore the consequences, while we were supposed to forget about them, and concentrate on our own chances for success.

Then came insecurities related to the body, when my father began to give it inappropriate attention, starting in my teens. My mother watched on instead of defending me, going as far as to behave as if I was "competition." I covered my body with forty pounds of extra flesh as a result towards the end of high school, succeeding only in creating patterns that took years to undo.

Intelligent action and development were expected of me, rather than encouraged or rewarded. To this day, I find it difficult to congratulate myself for being the problem-solver that I am, using my intuition as an extension of my senses. The joy I see in Tyler's eyes as I work around the house still hits a small blockade of arrogance on my part, planted in me early on in my family. "Of course I can do that," I want to say. But as valid for me is what he was often told as a kid: "Don't let it go to your head."

Later came the insecurity created by the diagnosis of a mental illness, twenty years ago. I had thrown my mind forward and neglected sleep and health, throwing my nervous system into a loop it did not recover from for a long time. It was my body that paid the price. Shame brought onto the family was made more important than recovery, until I insisted. A history of mental illness on both sides of the family was denied. I became the victim of choice.

Twenty years ago, psychotherapy was common in New York, but fully breaking with reality wasn't. The factor of pain was not entered in at the level that I experienced it. Feeling without security, without a sense of self, I was unable, at first, to regroup enough to stand on solid ground.

Two years ago, almost to the day, Tyler picked me up at the train station, and brought me here. He saw something I didn't, in me, and made the leap by taking me home. Now, with my sense of self reestablished, I can have faith in work coming as I need it.

Healing work sometimes involves removing barriers set for oneself first, including former self-imposed limitations. Degrees are incidental to leaving one's mark on the world. That sometimes involves consciously restoring the body's natural systems to a point from which they can repair themselves. Intent is important, as is taking one's own personality out of the equation as the work is being done.

It can be hard at first to accept that "saving" the person must not be the goal, since healing, as opposed to curing, is about connecting with the person at soul level, aiding in the intent of the soul, which may be different from the person's own desire. We tend to lose sight of this in a Western society in which survival of the body has become paramount, living as we do ruled by fear. I had to unlearn most of what I knew, to learn that.

As a child, I understood medicine through my parents, who were both doctors. I understood that they had special status as a result, and that they "fixed" people all day, every day. I got "fixed" too, first with eye exercises to correct my crossed eyes, then with four surgeries over the years to uproot benign tumours in my shoulder. Then my crushed knee, and my severed Achilles' tendon which somehow hung on but took me out of the running for any work that involves wearing heels. There was medication for an overactive thyroid, which was busy compensating for bipolar-related medication.

Eventually I made more time and prioritised my funds so I could begin to get clues to what would really work. Tyler established the platform for potential new security, Dr.Keyser led me through the quagmire or my own nervous system in a clinical sense, and I made time enough to integrate all helpful knowledge that has ever come my way. None of us will get better until we commit to our own health. I lost my fear in this way, trusting in common sense as my guide from now on.

I bring all of this to each massage, while understanding the responsibility of it. Making myself known actively is secondary. Painting is coming back too, after years during which that part of me was dead. Most of all, Tyler has created a home that I will not have to give up, a much-needed first for me. As long as I get my sleep, some exercise, and time to recover from situations that don't work for me, all is well. Redefinition, or fine-tuning, will continue the rest of my life, but the essential foundation is there so that a "total crash" scenario doesn't ever have to happen again.

I may continue to take lithium for the rest of my life, since I no longer live on the idyllic piece of land that allowed me to live without medication for a year in Canada; I may always have financial and emotional stress to unload daily in the life I live; but I will always be gathering myself daily now. Seeing the road ahead as it is, is preferable to staying in a daze and hoping for the best. It requires infinite patience to try, but even that can come in bite-size pieces.

As much as I might like to turn on the same switch for others, I can't until they let me in. "Fixing" is not part of what I do. I stand still, in a sense, whether my hands move or not, as healing passes through me. They have to do the work of allowing me in. Enough times I have to hold back internally and only wash general waves of warmth over tired muscles. Few are able to take the hint and continue the work on their own, but some do.

Cookie O'Puss is in bed with us again this morning, looking out the window through the chiffon curtain. I don't know what she can see, but her focus is enviable. From the edge of the bed, I see that the last of the leaves have fallen. Tyler and I both worked hard moving load after load to the curb. The heavy winds last night did the last of the job. There will be more kindling to pick up around the house, just in time.

Before I get out of bed, I take stock. My right shoulder is still in pain, deep into the chest. I am used to it. With yoga, it has gotten much better. For a week after the cranio-sacral class I had almost no pain at all, a direct credit to the technique. Finding out that there might have been something that would have brought release years ago, brings a sense of irony about it all. But it is so much more important now to just move on.

If anything, it is more obvious than ever that personal contact is more important. The more we all "cut corners", looking for the quick and easy way out, the more we get the caffeine jolts, get through faster, and then not know how to stop. I did that throughout art school, finishing in a mental collapse. Now, although I usually stop as soon as I feel myself slipping into rushed behaviour, I "pick and choose my battles," using up my reserves like some watch the gas gage go down to a critical level. I know the price I'll pay when I push, and mostly I choose not to, but when I do it is with the understanding that I will make time to regroup, mostly through rest, afterwards. Energy is conserved consciously with every move; I turn away work now, if I know any aspect of it is unhealthy for me beyond mild discomfort.

The same information filters down differently to all of us. In a time of mounting crisis globally, people expect the magic pill more than ever. Its major component, love, if anyone ever came up with it, is dismissed as naïve, possibly because it takes so much work, so much focus, so much attention, and sometimes standing by while others get the quick fix.

Could it be as easy for me as helping myself find a pattern of release that I can use as I need it, so that I can help others find their own? It seems so obvious and direct. My system gets triggered more readily, that is true. But I wonder more and more if that should be allowed to label me as mentally ill.

In Romania it is the custom to "fold in" moments of crisis as one might fold in an important component in a meal. Shock is absorbed, the person hopefully moves on. Both my parents did, after breakdowns in their early twenties. In the United States there is the stigma of the repressed, which doesn't end up creating a better-functioning society. "The norm", who ironically included my parents decades ago, would rather over-medicate those who have fallen and can't get up. Recovery takes much more energy.

Last night two couples came out ahead of us from a selective restaurant on the boulevard. We were walking back to where we parked for the night of wrestling. They knew more about wine than their waiter, it turned out, and were congratulating themselves for it. I was reeling from the sight of so much bruising for a full three hours. I might have looked more appropriate for the restaurant, despite trying my best to fit in, but given a choice I still would have picked the less pretentious atmosphere.

Behind me, a woman had been screaming during the match her son was in, so much so that I covered my right ear drum with my hand again, as I had the night before at the library. We had gone to see "The Invisible Man" and there was an issue with the soundtrack. My left ear has been dulled by years of phone use, in comparison.

There had been a resemblance between the crowd scenes in "The Invisible Man" and the crowd we were with. In both cases, it was the loss of personal identity that struck me. In between events a mother in front of us had been taking pictures of her young kids; we were emailing Tyler's brother. We reveled in our cheapest meal out ever: one dollar for a hot dog with trimmings, beans and kraut. But when the wrestling started, all of us blended in.

I agree with Tyler that wrestlers are among our modern-day gladiators, locally or nationally. There were cries to "fry the chicken" when a masked chicken man tried to hold his own. Someone wanted to give him leotard lessons so his underwear lines wouldn't show. At the end of the night, the crowd just stopped short of asking for blood. No one was taking any distance, from themselves or from what was going on. I reluctantly joined the raw feel of the place, being fully surrounded by it. The search for a moment of fame continues for so many, even at the risk of a lifetime of injury.

The crowd mourned a thirty-six-year-old-wrestler at the beginning of the night, then moved on. Football players get carted off the field during almost every game. I will not draw lines and say football is better. Winning or losing is still important, even if so much is agreed on to start with. When drawing for blood is the only way for a person to remember that they're alive, the best thing for me to do for myself is to step out of the way and let them get it elsewhere, like with my mother. Being out for a night of wrestling wasn't the best for me, nor is any contact with my mother, but I will "fold it in". My mother will return once more to the States at this point, before her final move back to Romania, and I will get through it. In February, Tyler and I will go back for more local wrestling and I will let the experience make me stronger.

I snapped today. After a morning of tension it was like the old days. I was given a gift card in resentment, not in earnest, and took offense at the caveat "don't open it right away." Like with much of my mother's old handouts, I wanted to be rid of this one as soon as possible. My brain was on fire as I drove towards home, stopped at the health food store, and later shopped at the grocery store with Tyler.

Tyler didn't understand this direct line to crash and burn, but he was able to reign in my need to waste, thankfully. Then we both swam, and it helped, like a cold compress on bruised muscles, but the injustice of a handout as opposed to an earned share lingered. A boss, whether at work or in one's family, can give themselves free reign to make brazen assumptions, also about how I will or will not move forward in my life financially. In return, being bent to crass biases is not an option for me.

With my mother's return days ago, I am almost grateful for having to stand up for my rights elsewhere. She forgave me, she said over the phone, for taking her driver's license away last fall. She gave me expensive perfume that she got at the duty free shop and was considering saving for my birthday; she gave Tyler a beautiful earthenware mug, and without skipping a beat announced that she would rent a room in our house while Tyler and I ate our chowder. She said she'll be moving to Romania before her lease runs out in June, so she'll need a physical address in the United States for several purposes, and we'd be it.

When she'd asked me to come get her at the airport, a few days before her return, she told me she would give me her new car as long as Tyler or I drive her around some. Yesterday the story shifted, and I put up a block, making it clear that she would never live in our house. After hours at her service, instead of giving me thanks she pulled out thirty bucks to give to me, thinking she would be done with that. I had taken the morning off from work to help her resolve a few things, and the thirty dollars would have almost covered that, but I didn't take it because I'm not actually driving Miss Daisy, as she likes to put it, but trying to reign in my mother's behaviour, or at least take good note of what is happening.

My mother told me that she and my sister agreed that as soon as she moves to Romania I can no longer claim to be responsible for my mother as I do now, since my sister will be geographically closer, but it still seem strange to me to be given the pink slip, a twenty at a time.

I still think of my father as my father, too, not a can of ashes, although my mother announced as brazenly that she would dig up my father's ashes and grave marking and drag both around Europe with her until her own death, so that both his and her ashes would be buried together, granite plaque and all, in my sister's back yard in Switzerland. I am not supposed to think about this either, because by then I will have been dismissed. This is the same woman who stayed at home to have her gas hooked up the morning of my father's burial, while my sister had already flown back to Switzerland.

After decades of both disdain and admitted hatred towards my father from both my mother and my sister, I find it hard to accept such a tremendous change of heart, and devotion. I will not understand, but I will not try to stop it, although in this I will not help at all either. If the desecration does take place, it will unfold at its own rate.

Despite our pain and differences, my father and I did have a bond that was something like love, and it will continue. My mother may have forgotten his express wish to be buried next to my grandmother. Or perhaps ashes are just crushed bones to her, just as living people's feelings are negligible.

Meanwhile my mother made it very clear that she feels she has no responsibility towards me. She made it clear yesterday that the monthly stipend that was set in place for me even before my father's death, gives her rights in her mind to my efforts and even my home. I am there to fix things and establish well-being, she is there to partake. I had to clarify that what I thought of also as my father's money, does not buy me.

My mother reassured me that all of my father's money is now hers, and she is in no way obligated to help me. Then I reminded her that I gave her seven years of my life free of charge, during which I took care of both of them. Faced with that, she said that if I felt that I'd earned it, she would continue to "give me" the stipend as long as she can afford to.

Years ago my father had insisted that their house come to me after their death, long before his final descent into dementia. He wanted me looked after. Since it's easy to dismiss that, and all my help in the sale of their home when the time came, it becomes easier to understand how my mother can neglect my father's request to be allowed to rest in peace finally next to my Nonna in Westfield.

I have pockets of meaningful work to look forward to these days, though for a gambler like my mother only the big bucks count, not a concerted manageable effort. She would even have me assign a charge to putting numbers into the new cell phone she wanted. What I can do for my mother counts for her in dollars and cents only, maybe with coaching from my sister who undoubtedly still thinks I would "cost less" in Romania.

My mother would establish fees, haggle over them, and proceed to call herself my "cash cow" with every check. At the same time, she informed me and the guy at the phone store that I should count myself lucky to have a mother to do things for. It is practically entrapment, or would be if I fell for it, of a psychological kind. She saves soft words for strangers, and lets me have center stage in her menagerie of psychoses. I am glad to have survived my life with her, to experience so much clarity and not feel that I must rescue her before I can live for myself.

Later in the day I was relieved that I insisted on my mother's not driving anymore, seeing how disoriented she is even on local streets as a passenger. My father dipped this quickly too, he out of illness, she out of an apparent toxic need to pollute and dominate, from words to cigarettes, which have been confirmed to worsen the macular degeneration in her one good eye.

I will step back and let it unfold this time, taking the car if she still means it, but without insisting. If it doesn't happen there will be another solution when the engine in my own car finally seizes sometime in the near future.

Things are still coming out of left field on this latest ride with my mother, like her saying over lunch with Tyler yesterday that if we looked hard enough at the place mats at the Chinese restaurant next time we go, we should be able to find out that we are incompatible in our natures and should break up. Two years into our relationship, she would still pour acid in our food. She thought it would be a nice thing Tyler could do the next time he wants to upset me. All of this seems strange to both me and Tyler, after our trying so hard to welcome her into our lives. Her jokes aren't funny, they're not even jokes.

I'm being fired as a daughter, this time in less uncertain terms than in the past when my usefulness might have seemed more attractive. My mother wants to keep her option open, though, to draw on my compassion again in the future, as if all the demeaning, abusive actions on her part in the past could be waved away, even by pity.

My mother would rent me here and there, as it were. No inheritance, no stipend perhaps even, just a pay-by-the-hour daughter. Perhaps it is all a joke, or as Tyler's father once told him, a big damn joke.

Some people have children out of love, others, like medieval European farmers, because they need more hands for work in the fields. My mother chose my sister as a daughter and me as a servant and it went from there.

At the airport, my mother's first move was to go outside for a smoke immediately. Through the glass, she pointed her one good eye at me as I stood inside with her luggage cart. In the car, she pointed out right away that I am healthy, beautiful, but not wealthy, though she forgot to mention wise. Early on, she must have got it into her head that everything is for sale, most of all beauty, and for awhile while I was focusing on helping her with my father, my mother kept insisting that I should cash in on my looks while I still have them, perhaps never expecting that to happen. When I fell for Tyler and he for me, much less to do with looks than she might like, the joke turned on her, and she has been uncomfortable about it since. I earn my keep, and that makes it worse. Thus this renewed need to belittle, perhaps.

I had had small hopes before her return that she might come to her senses in a compassionate way and extend real help to me, and us, financially, at this difficult time. At a time when the whole country is in dire straits, so am I, but with dignity and enough to get by, while my mother is not at all in need yet, despite her extensive gambling. But with all that has just happened, I will now turn away, take my severance pay if there is any, and move on, knowing that a healthy parent would not behave the way my mother has behaved. She doesn't have patience to hide her motives anymore now, she just wants me off the premises. I have waited for what might be fair, proud as I am, but it is finally time to close that door and leave her behind it to fend for herself.

This year I will not celebrate my birthday with my friends, because I will have to concentrate on this final battle in my epic war with my mother. I am proud to have survived long enough to know that all I needed was to survive my mother. I can become more than financially stable on my own merits, that I know. I had been waiting in vain for perhaps one last try at reconciliation. My father released me through his death, my mother is releasing me crassly in life. On my fortieth birthday, my father was still alive, and knowing that no celebration for me would be forthcoming I cooked a decent meal for a few of us on my father's birthday instead, two weeks before mine. Now I can look forward to a future birthday celebration that will be free of debris.

In the midst of heavy activity, I know well enough to stop and catch my breath. I notice that I still expect to be reprimanded by Tyler, whom I sometimes unfairly assign as my authority figure, for doing something as harmless as buying myself a guitar on my own birthday. When the reprimand doesn't come, when love and support come instead, I understand a little more what a deep mark was left by my father.

I have talked about how Tyler's love thaws out long-neglected aspects of my being: not just my mind, not just my emotions, not even just my body, but a greater whole, which is connected to something more. If I were a wrestler in the ring, this would be the last minute of the match, my being pinned down by the sum of my own experiences to date, having to make the final effort to reverse the situation.

The level of warrior experience in me allows for my will to carry now past illusions of ever having had a nurturing mother. Tyler and CookieO'Puss stand with me, as do all my friends. All is in place for me to take the last step to freeing myself: calm action, deliberate in the intent of healing myself, as the last of my frozen limbs undergo regeneration.

There was a time when it was essential to shut parts of myself off so as to survive, now it is just as important to "fold" these forgotten parts back in. I never counted on that kind of intense renewal, although a natural instinct of survival was there all along. This won't be as easy as being put under for an operation since I'll have to stay awake, but it will come.

My mother says she isn't needed anymore here in the States, so she will go to live near her brother, who does need help. She reminded me that, according to her, I used to be "in and and out of hospitals" and that she was needed then, but not now. The last cycle of hospitalisation was over in 1999, with a minor recurrence in 2002 after which the doctor on the ward told me to go home and stop fighting with my mother.

When my father died, I had been completely "clean" for five years already, but my mother even now blends my life before Tyler into one wavering hospitalisation, during which time she was always needed. I couldn't help notice the link, as if my health and my happiness are now an affront to her.

If my mother had indeed forgiven me over the license issue as she said before her return, some of this might have made me uncomfortable now. Instead, I am relieved. The sulking approach she took today as I drove her around no longer touched me. We know where we stand. If she could, she would harm me now, in punishment, but it doesn't sink in anymore. Being given notice of termination as a daughter is turning out to be what was needed.

There is no better way to break a dependence than to have it broken for me. I used to need to be useful too, toward my family, until I was shunned by most of them last fall for daring to confront my mother abruptly over her driving. Meanwhile I have learned that I am capable of living fully on my own, with encouragement from Tyler and various friends. Now that I do, seemingly more every day, my ability to function well is a given, as is my sanity. For nearly two years, my mother has taken my living fully as such, though she has done a lot to thwart it.

Few know that until this last return of hers I was moving

forward by sheer will, internally, holding on mostly to the resentment that had kept me "in place" all this time. With the last violent emotional amputation of being told that I am my mother's daughter only because I am still in her will, I am finally letting all the resentment of the past return to its source and stepping out of the way.

Time and distance are often needed to get a fresh look. Clarity this time came from realizing that I have learned my mother's ways over the years and lived them, without their ever being my own. But learned behaviour is not natural instinct, and can be unlearned.

It is not in my nature to destroy a person so that I may feel well, worthy, etc. When I have engaged in destructive combat with my mother, which she would have me do again now, I was using her skills. Now I would only mirror what she does. There is a difference.

My mother's current crystallized obsession with instilling at least some guilt in me, has shown me that, having found my own nature, I must not expect others to act outside of their own. My mother has finally severed the umbilical chord by showing me that she doesn't feel compelled to show compassion towards me at all, despite my being of her own flesh. I will have to get my emotional milk elsewhere.

My mother's perception of me, however, will continue to be limited by her need to dominate. Now I can consider this a trait of the elderly and let it go. Living with the reality of such a limited perception on her part, I will censor myself so as not to rock her frail reality other than to mirror her behaviour as she lashes out.

A Pokemon birthday card for me from my mother came in the mail, warning me to prepare for a duel. But there will be no duel. A Great Dane could step forcefully onto the head of any pocketbook dog and crush it, but it would not be in the nature of a Great Dane to do so. In a similar way, my own nature will not encourage further combat with my mother.

Besides, it is snowing peacefully on the day before my birthday. My cat is sitting with me on the couch, wishing I would not go to work this morning, as she would like me to stay home every morning when I'm getting ready for work. It is lovely that she wants me home so much, especially in the quiet of the morning, when she can tune into me best and send me all her love.

After a bath late last night, my love was brushing my hair on the couch as we listened to some vintage Stones, complete with a skip in the record. Garrett knows every one of these songs. Soon my replacement strings for my new guitar will come, and I will ask him to teach me how to play. I look forward to hearing my own voice again, which I've kept to a minimum since high school. Unhampered by the desire to be anyone other than who I am, I will be adding more rhythm to my life in yet another way.

Tyler and I patch each other up cyclically, often being battered by people we used to trust. He sends me out into the world, always telling me to be careful. Ireland will wait. Though we would know what to do with the experience, and would carry it with us for the rest of our lives, as we did Sighisoara, we cannot afford it. There is no shame in that, just sorrow. Time flies, but there is the last battle to walk away from, for now.

Now I can understand why so many people other than Tyler shy away from getting in the way of my mother's fiery brain on my behalf. They know they would just be consumed in the fire. At times I've gushed affection or compassion disproportionately because I was encouraged not to spare my own energy by my father, then by my mother. Now I know restraint, and it makes sense, mine and others'. When my mother's temper will doubtless flare over dinner tonight, I will survive it, if nothing else.

Having studied my mother's rage so well, I can understand it, though I cannot condone it. She learned suppression in her own life, but not restraint, so she can't "act in a calm and cultured manner" now, as they put it in Recovery, Inc. terms. At the doctor's office last week, her temper exploded and left a mark. As I prepare for tonight, I remind myself that I am a human being who contributes positively to this world. I will survive the situation because my physical body will carry me.

Camille Claudel's family stripped her of her studio and all of her work with the death of her father. Her own brother, a celebrated French poet, stood by as her mother put Camille away for life in a mental hospital and insisted that she never be allowed to touch clay again. She had been Rodin's student, then mistress, then adversary when her own work became as notable as his own. She was swept under the national rug for having been an embarrassment of manic and depressive rages for years before her father's death. He had refused to cut her off, despite everything.

Camille Claudel is celebrated around the world as a genius in our day. I came across her in my last year at Cooper, ironically as my own brain was on fire and headed for a crash. She was a strong warning to be sure, but I had already lost control of the brakes in my own emotional life. My father wanted fame for me, not excuses. Time ran out.

Now I make a point of putting things off, when it's time for dinner, time for sleep. Jobs had to be finished well and quickly years ago, with no room for error. A crushing sense of failure, including depression and anxiety, would follow any mishap. Success brought only temporary relief but no sense of accomplishment. Expectations ran too high.

Over dinner last night, Tyler lovingly offered my mother proud news of my having cooked a fully delicious meal in our kitchen the night before, for the first time ever. My mother made a dismissive remark. We complimented her on her new haircut and suit but she only glared back. She had been noticing my beautiful black dress that I had also worn a year before for my birthday party in Romania. She asked where I got it and said that it looked beautiful on me.

Then Tyler overstepped her recent rude behaviour and invited her for dinner at our home on Sunday, though it had been established that she would not be welcome to ever live with us. She let loose that she wouldn't, because, she said, I had told her that I couldn't to have her under the same roof with me at all. I protested for a moment, she protested back, then Tyler quickly stepped in, but the damage was done. She had drawn life directly out of me again.

I was stunned at the accusation, with my first instinct being to wrestle some sense into my mother. That gave way very quickly, in silence, to my coming to see that trying to clear my name would have been pointless. Those who would believe my mother's fabrications would believe this one too. In the same way that I believe fighting covert terrorism with armed forces only fuels its growth, I have to stand as best I can now and repair the new damage.

Just after midnight, Tyler came into our bedroom where

I had retreated, soon after we got home from dinner. There he was, with enough lit candles on my birthday cake to jolt me back into being. He had presents waiting for me in the living room at the foot of our Christmas tree. It is still well and speaks of regeneration through its very presence. Tyler saw the damage done and lent me his will so I would have a chance.

        Like some physical therapists manipulate limbs in difficult recovery cases, Tyler pulled at my whole being despite both our pain, and would not let go. His Viking warmth acted as balm where it was needed, which was everywhere. Two days later, I am able to consider more again, almost fully restored. Love came to me in the form of my man, not of any illusion of my past. Gratitude is not a big enough word for what I feel. Thank you, my love, will do, only because he understands there's so much more. The chapter ends, we take a breath together and move on.

8.

Yesterday it was a young veteran in gear standing outside of Pathmark instead of Girl Scouts selling cookies. It was a cold day. He came in to buy some warm food while we were winding up our shopping. He wished us a good day on our way out. His face showed experience without rancour; he had the look of the initiated, of those who know they can't go back to a prior stage of their lives. He didn't seem to expect donations or thanks. He seemed to know he had done enough. The fact that he was still in uniform suggested to me that he might return for another rotation, not belonging as much now to the world of civilians.

I am forced to consider again how much of our lives is about competition. Alan Watts said there should always be conflicts, given our human nature, but not of an absolute kind. We need enemies, but not to the point of extermination. With my uncle's death, my mother remarked that she is used to having life deal her dirty tricks. She had hoped to spend several years with him, in moving to Romania this coming summer. I had thought of Kiki's death as a release from life-long pain, but kept my silence towards my mother so as not to seem disrespectful. My grandmother left us suddenly too, having told us for years that she would go painlessly in her sleep, as she did. I saw that as an affirmation of Nonna's wisdom, my mother didn't.

On Oscar night, the country is willing to lose itself in the superficiality of gowns and gossip. The WFMU marathon is on too, asking for help in postponing what might be inevitable: the death of independent radio. The party is on. At our house, Tyler has been cooking Irish: corned beef and trimmings today, shepherd's pie the other night of which about half is left. I will try to introduce reason to my mother tonight by having her meet Melania. The chances are small that she would accept Melania as a live-in companion, but in many ways it seems the most logical choice, to me.

A woman beeped behind us today although we were going at the speed limit and a red light was coming up. What I've been reading about healing encourages me to have an inclusive outlook when people are rude or short-sighted, but jarring differences between ideal behaviour and what is at best careless indifference are still upsetting even now. At home, our cat was snuggled on the couch, the house smelled of Ireland, and balance was quickly restored. The events of the coming week will wait as we enjoy our reprieve from the world.

The initiated know the "dirty trick" secret well: something is taken away and cannot be replaced. Either the knowledge that one has crossed the line of taking a life, or the understanding that some insults go so deep that they can never be scrubbed out of consciousness. We learn to be watchful, at best, and to stop ourselves from being truthful or sincere until certain assurances are made. As a result, time is taken up daily with building trust so that minute exchanges of value can happen. It is in those moments that we are reassured, and move forward internally.

      I have squandered much of my energy as I've moved through destructive and regenerative cycles of my own creative life. I've shown too much emotion, swallowed guilt that wasn't mine, and stood as still as possible as others left their mark on me, as some do on the bark of trees. My mother is trying to leave a deep mark again now, by telling me that she is moving back to Romania because I took away her freedom. She will not allow me to dissuade her from what I see as a dangerous decision, or to take any part in her life once she's moved, but I am to be held accountable for any ill that becomes her there. That is more of what in PRH, the writing therapy group I took part in so many years ago in Canada, is called "crazy-making" behaviour.

      I look for my relief in meditation, early in the morning in bed, and while swimming laps at the pool. After a day's work, the tension in my muscles dissolves almost the moment I enter the water. Lately I have been swimming more, with ease, so that there is a training factor too now, where there used to be just musing. I'm in a period of proving something to myself again, in a constructive way this time.

      The easy thing would be to deny healthy needs of my own and devote much of my life to my mother again now, despite that helpless feeling of being drained emotionally and physically from day to day. Taking the time to strengthen my body and my relationship with Tyler instead goes directly against the grain of what I've known so far. Balance, faith and belief in myself are becoming real in a way which cannot be denied, and which require direct involvement on my part. I've never cared about being a contender, nor would I now, but I am willing finally to celebrate my gifts.

      Guilt will not give my mother entry into our home now, as she would like it to. I have become ill in the past directly because of her physical presence or psychological influence, and I will not allow it anymore, more so since it turns out to be just a pointless exercise in control on her part. My first responsibility is to myself. Destructive behaviour will no longer be allowed to disturb the balance that I took so long to build. Humour and goodwill will win this war of attrition.

      When I see families in which war is not a way of life, I wander why I've allowed it to be mine, all this time. Tyler's playfulness and love have intervened in the last two-and-a-half years, allowing me to regroup in a way that lets me consider an existence not based on continual emergencies, expectations, and demeaning behaviour, which are based on manipulation through money. My mother is slamming the money gavel again now, no matter what harm it brings to me. It is the ultimate irony in retrospect, since my mother and father had insisted that they defected to the United States to gives me and my sister our freedom. Now my mother would keep me on a leash, as she would have me starve my cat when she is being finicky about food.

   As an experienced swimmer survives violent waves on the ocean, I will survive this time in my life. I often look forward to moments days from now as well as at what is happening now, using another Recovery, Inc. spotting of "anticipating joyfully or not at all." When positive contact is reaffirmed in new work relationships, new positive grooves take the place of old ruts. This is a painful process in itself, but it works, with diligent application.

   Last night I knew that if I held on to Tyler's arm I would make it home, feed CookieO'Puss and then sink my pained body into a hot bath, that everything would be alright then, and it was. Full recovery will take days, but whereas my body would have collapsed years ago, asking to be taken to the nearest emergency room, now I trusted in restful sleep, toast and hot chocolate to bring me around. My stomach, as it is for many, is the seat of all emotional turmoil, though it might have been the hamburger too, or the exhaustion of coping with the weekend flood. Once more my body said no more, rest.

   This time exhaustion went beyond that gentle state of acceptance in which no amount of energy is wasted. There are times when I can push. Last night I couldn't. Although the collective memory of others who have gone through hardship before sustains me, this time I went too far. But by tomorrow I may be able to return to a full meal, and function with only a nap in the afternoon. Not rushing is a given now, but clearly other major adjustments are to follow.

   With this willingness to adjust in place, I am ready to listen to the lives of others. Through them I put my own events in perspective. I know fully that I can't project my own importance without falling flat on my face, so I find myself editing my need to step beyond compassion into meddling, willing to stand the frustration of helplessness.

   The old arrogance that "I know better" would still surface, when indeed I don't know better and could never direct other lives. People with sensitive nervous systems love to "fix" others, another thing that was pointed out so clearly for me by Dr.Low of Recovery, in his writings. The title of his most basic book, Mental Health Through Will Training, makes the need for self-restraint evident.

   Now, patience through an effort of the will keeps my muscles still when I might be compelled to get what I want on the spot. The communal racing thoughts of our society at this time would add to mine, if I let them. The instant solution is always looming but never comes. My mother won't win the lottery, but her addiction to gambling will assure that she'll always try. The fact that she doesn't hold herself responsible for her own behaviour means that I can't hold her responsible for it either. Still my body weakens with the effort to make it all make sense. "The inevitable setback" mentioned often in Recovery is part of the "total view" for me at this time.

Perfection stopped being a requirement in my life long ago, but I still find myself taking care of others' needs before my own, in all capacities. When my body does break down, it becomes clear that I have to stand the discomfort of not meeting all the needs others have of me. In other words, that I don't need "outer approval," another key Recovery term. After forty years of dogged family indoctrination about self-effacement, I have no choice but to stand proud.

Two girls ran ahead of their father toward the parking lot. The younger one stumbled and fell, scraping her knee on the pavement. The older one still wanted her hot chocolate, which her father was carrying for her. When he caught up with them, the father threw the hot chocolate he had been carrying violently onto the ground as a lesson to the older girl for not showing concern for the younger, reprimanded both, and moved on with both girls to their car in a show of temper. I had no choice but to respect the "tough love" approach, in the same way that I had to accept the choice of a friend to lock a disobedient cat in the basement one evening when we were invited to dinner. It is possible that somewhere in her mind my mother might still only be disciplining me too, unaware of her abusive behaviour.

That my mother refuses to seek psychiatric help now, declaring that she is no longer depressed because she no longer takes medication for it, is more dangerous. The anger that has replaced her depression, the rages she indulges in towards me, are potent substitutes for depression from the point of view of Recovery, but they imply a constant need for more. She would spend my energies in her need to survive in this way, but I will not allow it. I remind myself that I am not responsible for all her troubles if only because I was born after her, not before her, and that her depression came long before mine.

I am forced also to notice again that my mother's frustration with my sister goes unsatisfied, because my sister has always nodded her head but done whatever she wanted to anyway, leaving my mother to try to dominate me. I have tried to absorb and cushion some of my mother's rage these past months, but the stark clarity of her most recent rudeness leads me to a simple conclusion: I need a vacation. Cindy mentioned it first, as a word of caution; now I will heed her warning. Guilt, my mother's final frontier, need not crush me.

"Be Happy, Be Healthy, Belong" said a sign outside a public building. I liked the fun in it, hoping it was not supposed to compel in a way other than humorous. I had just been listening to Alan Watts in the car, talking about belonging in our own lives, so the slogan was an uncanny affirmation.

There is no sign of the light nature or spirit of Chinese culture in the restaurant I've stopped to get spring rolls in. The people here are busy surviving, polite and effective but no more. I am keeping to my schedule too, but have made time to eat, rest and reflect. On a beautiful, cool spring day, I feel like I belong in my life. Accepting harmlessness as a way of life is becoming easier.

Days ago Jill's simple observation released another lock that had long been in place: that I have a lot of problems, but none of them are mine. In other words, that I have taken on the burdens of others. I function well, listen to advice, support myself, and stand by my man and my friends. But, until now, I have taken on the limitations of others as my own, including insecurities, biases, and pain. Returning more and more to thoughts of my twelfth year, before the deluge of facts concerning events that were out of my control, I see that I have taken on so much that wasn't mine.

Over the past thirty years there have been many times when it might have been easier not to struggle, but to accept myself as mentally ill to the point of being unable to function. My family could have felt sorry for themselves then and thrown away the key. But something would not give way, and it has come to this: my problems weren't mine to begin with. It was the patterns that were set in place by trying to make them mine, that derailed me.

I have borrowed problems so as to have purpose. My father needed to involve me in his need for affection, encouraging me to develop insecurities that would maintain a cycle of self-doubt. He did not dominate my mother, so he would dominate me. I have chosen father-like men in relationships time and again, trying to solve the riddle for myself. Now something even more impossible than a Gordian knot came unwound, with that simple remark, without force. I can look to myself, finally, over thirty years later.

What drew me in toward my father initially was his own vulnerability. He needed an ally against the world, and I as his golden child was willing to distract him from it. Later his Jekyll and Hyde contortions made him unbearable and brought jealousy from my mother, but there was no escape for me. I would be encouraged by him in my artwork, then have to bear the lecherous glances that he indulged in towards me. He needed me to win where he had lost, to find success in the world, but no man could touch me, especially not near the end of his life. About my first boyfriend, when I was seventeen, he said "I know what I'd do with you if I were thirty years younger!" That set the tone for my adult relationship with my father.

As time went on I put my independence in hock so I could get some skills in the world, putting up with the bitter language of guilt and servitude. Now, after all these years, my mother is trying her last best shot at what used to work, and I have the audacity to change the rules. Only, it is as if something more has fallen away from me than disregard, or reneging on old obligations. Contracts that were written in blood long ago are dispelled not because I would not stand by them if I still felt them to be true, but because they were a hoax to begin with.

They were a hoax because love is not by nature conditional. My mother would have control now, dismissing love, although the old pattern has fallen away. She would have me waste myself away as I did for my father when he had become helpless and in need of compassion. Now my mother is demanding her pound of flesh, and it's not working. He had my respect, long ago, had made some attempt to earn it before leaving Romania for good, while my mother never did. She had always chosen instead to put me in my place. Too delicate, she would say, and still does. She would still ask me to be other than what I am.

But I slipped through her fingers, and now have the effrontery to act with concern and responsibility towards her. And here, at this moment, on a cold spring afternoon, I have the clarity to know that as a daughter I have done all I needed to do and more, that I do not owe hours of service for accepting a car I did not trick her out of, as she would have me believe. I can be certain that I can't put a dam on behaviour so reckless in terms of disregard for one's own health, also that my mother's need for attention in that respect is a game and no more. Nothing I do would give my mother a stroke, as she has accused me of, recently. That her body can't sustain life much longer at its current rate of abuse cannot be my fault. Living for myself can't be a crime, and isn't. The days of my servitude are over.

Ironically I stayed a servant until that revelation: with so much at stake for my own well-being, I have, until recently, assumed the responsibility for my mother's well-being, if not happiness. As long as I believed that her problems were mine, they were mine. In the past months, she's told me that I'm not her daughter anymore except in name, but she required all the old-world respect a mother would have at the same time, nearly convincing me back into the old possessive loop of guilt of my father's days. And yet, her problems are her own.

starting at fourteen, paying the mortgage and the bills. People don't understand, some don't approve. Being initiated so young, he chose to live his life instead of minding winding tongues. He held on to our home in the process, and developed fully into the writer and photographer that he is.

It would not be like Tyler to waste resources, as my mother does on gambling. A budget is important, as is living by it. The total lack of restraint that my mother would want to experience desperately now, that I have known time and again, is to Tyler an indulgence to be avoided and no more. I admire that, and have come to see that most material possessions require cautious consideration. That extends for me now to a healthy weariness regarding glamorous aspects of the world around me, from television to fads, to attitudes.

In our home there are always more projects to be taken on, another gift which might seem a burden to others. Every task for me is a physical show of a mental unwinding, a much-needed form of relaxation. Yesterday I nicked the casing for the position light on the new car as I put my table into the trunk. Today I spent the time to scoop the plastic shards out of the light chamber, and improvised a solution when one of them fell irretrievably into the casing of the light, putting it all back together with epoxy. By tomorrow the glue will have set completely, leaving me with a mark of my ingenuity and confidence in myself. Red nail polish will finish the job, with thanks to Dr.Low for the "spotting" that "Perfection is a hope, a dream, and an illusion."

Each day at home, with all the little jobs, wears away at old grooves of perfectionism. I take my naps, I write my notes, I prepare for the next day, and for the rest of the time events move with fluidity. Whereas in the old days I needed to finish everything on a daily basis because of the dread of unknown new burdens the following day, now it is nice to look forward to what might have to be put off for weeks, like sewing up the cushions of the armchair in the new room. The time will come when I will need that dreamy concentration of a few hours, but not yet.

Now, having to consider the opinions and wishes of others without confrontation is a joy, since every issue addressed without a temperamental reaction reaffirms the possibility of resolution without temper. That flies directly in the face of what I've known in my family all my life, but the muck of it all might settle yet, leaving a clear mountain lake to bathe in.

Oppression lifts internally, but the change shows right away. There is no weight now to my mother's decision to join us for Easter dinner or not. If she does come, she will be rude. Tyler, who has seen enough abuse at her hand these past few months, would still have her at our table, since he knows how important Easter is in Romania. I respect his wish, whether she accepts the invitation or not. The vacation I hoped for is already happening for me internally, though actual absence through time will be very welcome. My mother would tear me down; I would have her live out her God-given days, but not at my expense.

The shift brings clarity in another respect: adjusting out of the refugee approach. As much as my parents didn't want me and my sister to have to relive their youths, once the sacrifice of bringing us to the United States was made, a refrain was set in place that was to always remind us of what was owed my parents for the effort. The debt established was in fact never to be surmounted. I hadn't known refugee ways before, and felt trapped in a life I had not asked for.

A cycle of guilt took hold. To escape the accusation of "having it easy" I overstepped from altruism into seeing to the needs of others only. Not being deprived materially by my family, I was nonetheless deprived of living out my generous nature when it meant extending it outside the family.

In time this led to erratic spending, which fell in nicely as a symptom of manic depression. It was however more a result of crazy-making behaviour in the family, being told that indeed I am an artist who will need to roam the earth in search of experience, but not on their dime. In the gutter indeed, on a night the stars weren't out. The more I struggled, having tasted the need for what would lead to an independent spirit, the more I caught myself up, all the time being reminded of what others had to do without.

What Robin told me twenty years ago, that I should put aside painting and get a job, was true. But at the time I had entered so deep into the quagmire of self-doubt that I believed it when I was told in the family that I was permanently damaged, that I had sullied the family reputation, that no man would want me, nor would any boss hire me. Surviving that compounded attitude, along with experimental drugs to render me functional, took all my energy for years, until PRH, Recovery, therapy, and finally the leap of faith of one man.

Tyler was saddled with a refugee approach to life early on by both his parents, but he turned their approach into a life full of experience. Through good planning he was able to travel for twenty years, swim most days, read, and keep up with some of the paintings he loves in New York every winter, renewing himself in the ocean every summer. That was after he worked for twenty straight years after his father's death,

In the gray of the rain this morning, I listen to Linda as I drive to work. Tomorrow will be Tyler's sixtieth birthday, and sunny. For the time being a gray commuter train passes as I wait for the light to turn green. Buds on the trees don't have enough pigment to cut through a colourless curtain of wind. We have had more snow this winter than ever, now more rain in March than ever, but some would still believe nothing has changed in terms of weather patterns. On the drive back there's more, and a rare headache comes on.

If the Volvo is not toast, I will pass it on for a fair price. It is alright to let go of it now, of all the hopes my mother had for my success with it. It is time to let go of the last the arrogance I might have associated with it for myself, still proving something. What's left will go towards a brake job for the ancient Tercel, and anything else it needs. When I do pay off my credit cards, I will close the accounts I have and only use the one through my bank. I am surprised that so much more ambition is falling away from me now, but I am relieved at the same time.

I thought for awhile that I would need to maintain a certain lifestyle for us through my efforts, but it turns out that I don't. Tyler refused to let me splurge on his birthday yesterday, and he is consistent in his approach. Having no guilt, I adopted the guilty habits of my family instead, thinking that I should make a show of abundance, according to the "noblesse oblige" concept that my mother has pronounced flawlessly at intervals, usually with mocking irony.

Here I am though, as we both recover from the long day yesterday, from my aching knee and the long walk home in the middle of the night, carrying our heavy books from The Strand. Past one in the afternoon, there is no better place to be than next to Tyler, who's snoring softly in his McSorleys' t-shirt, with CookieO'Puss at our feet shielding her eyes with her paw as she waits patiently to be fed, and my own fleece blanket wrapped around me. My tired legs will recover by tomorrow, and I may find my old knee brace, later on.

The irony of so much instilled anxiety finally dissolving is something I'll take any day over a jackpot. The Catch 22 of having to find it out for myself was the nagging issue that would not let go; now I have been initiated. Until now I could not say that, because I always went back and forth, wanting justice and explanations. No one step was ever completed, and even to think of something being completed now may be premature.

I may drown yet with my first gulp of a different kind of breath than I'm used to. Then again, I may not. The afternoon will bring a reality of errands and the sight of nothing where two neighbouring trees used to be, but there is the presence of something which will not be taken away, now.